SONGS OF RELIGION AND LIFE.

SONGS

OF

RELIGION AND LIFE

BY

JOHN STUART BLACKIE

PROFESSOR OF GREEK IN THE UNIVERSITY OF EDINBURGH

NEW YORK

SCRIBNER, ARMSTRONG & CO.

1876.

John F. Trow & Son,
Printers and Bookbinders,
205–213 *East 12th St.*,
NEW YORK.

PREFACE.

THE Poems in this volume may be regarded as a Second Edition of the second part of my 'Lays and Legends of Ancient Greece,' which has long been out of print, along with other Poems not hitherto published, and a few from a volume of 'Lyrical Poems' previously published, all having a common object, viz., the cultivation of religious reverence without sectarian dogmatism, and of poetical sentiment tending not so much to amuse the imagination or to tickle the fancy as to purify the passions and to regulate the conduct of life. That the composition of these Poems, as occasion offered, has been a source of intellectual enlargement and of moral elevation to myself I am well convinced; and I am not without hope that they may act as a salutary stimulus to others, who know that there is one thing needful, viz., the formation of a noble character, and that everything else is vanity. As for the philosophy that lies at the bottom of these Poems—and all true poetry is a concrete philosophy,—it is only a modern expression of the Nineteenth Psalm, recognising, as that noble composition does, the essential unity and divine significance alike of the physical world without and the moral world within, as a glorious biform manifestation of the great uncaused Cause of the Universe,—an altogether different wisdom—at once more profound and more complete—from that meagre dissection and tabulation of the soulless outside of things which, with a forward display of knife and microscope, has in these latter days been palmed off upon us for a philosophy. But it is too late in the day to set up Epicurus on the throne of Plato, however the advocates of our monkey-brotherhood may delight themselves, and amuse a few gaping people, by turning things outside in and upside down for a season.

JOHN S. BLACKIE.

EDINBURGH, *December* 1875.

In Him we live and move and have our being.

ST. PAUL.

The Kingdom of Heaven is within you.

I. H. S.

In Christ Jesus there is neither circumcision nor uncircumcision, but a new creature. ST. PAUL.

CONTENTS.

Songs of Religion.

b

In Him we live and move and have our being.
ST. PAUL.

The Kingdom of Heaven is within you.
I. H. S.

In Christ Jesus there is neither circumcision nor uncircumcision, but a new creature. ST. PAUL.

CONTENTS.

Songs of Religion.

Songs of Life.

Songs of Religion.

Advent-Hymn.

LO, He comes!—Messiah neareth,
Jesus comes;
Not with pomp the God appeareth,
Meek He comes.
Pride displays no blazoned banners,
Vanity no false, fair manners,
Where He comes.

Not with Conqueror's ring and rattle,
Wild war's glee,
Ushered by a bloody battle,
Cometh He.
As the West wind's gentle blowing
Wakes life's mystic power of growing,
Thus doth He.

Cæsar, 'mid thy legions' thunder,
Dost thou hear?
Hark! from Heaven a hymn of wonder
Full and clear:—
'Open wide the blissful portals,
Peace on Earth, goodwill to Mortals!'
Charms the ear!

Rome, beneath thy glittering armour,
Grimly gored,
Iron Mother, bloody charmer,
Sheathe the sword!
Shall thy natal wolf still claim thee?
Lo! I send a power to tame thee,
Saith the Lord.

Forms of vain will-worship mumbling,
Priests, have done!
Creeds with creeds incongruous jumbling,
Know the one!

See the end of all confusion,
Common truth of all delusion,
    In the SON!

Vainly sundering walls thou raisest.
    Pharisee!
Orthodox in vain thou praisest
    Bound to thee!
Nought is isolated, single,
All in brothered rays do mingle
    Under Me.

Subtle Doctors sagely fooling
    Humankind,
With crude dogmas harshly schooling
    Infant mind,
Kick the solemn architecture!
Vainly shall a blind director
    Lead the blind.

Wise men, something still conceiving
Like the true,
Busy brains still idly weaving
Something new,
Like a star in strength upshooting,
I the end of all disputing
Show to you!

Gape not! gaze not! I display not
Dazzling shows;
With loud logic I gainsay not
Wrangling foes.
Noiseless victories ye shall win you!
Seed Heaven-planted—look within you,
There it grows!

Little seed! thy hidden virtue
Stirs Time's womb;
The bright promise thou art heir to
Lights the tomb:

Now the unvalued dust thee covers,
Soon, the sought of many lovers,
Thou shalt bloom.

Simple Truth! while brilliant blunders
Fools achieve,
Thou thy quiet chain of wonders
Wisely weave:
Where strong hate to love surrenders,
From the strife that pride engenders,
Work reprieve.

From the hard rock let the fountain
Blithely dart!
Cleave the foul mist, move the mountain,
Faithful heart!
Let the stony frozen regions
Blush with life by high religion's
Magic art!

Kings shall own thee; knaves shall use thee;
    Fools despise;
Babbling Doctors shall confuse thee,
    Witless wise:
Rival sages shall, in duty,
On thy common web of beauty,
    Stamp their dyes.

Go! and, though my hope deceive me,
    In thy plan
I will hope; I will believe thee
    While I can.
Go and conquer!—If thou win not,
Earth may crack, and GOD will sin not
    Cursing MAN.

John the Baptist.

WHO is he in hairy raiment
Clad, i' the wilderness
Preaching freely without payment
Truth and righteousness?
Whoso hears and not despises,
Him with water he baptises,
In the contrite hour;
Whoso hears with haughty scorning,
Him he smites with holy warning,
And with prophet's power.

Swarms the city from its corners,
Motley bad and good;
Thoughtless hearts and heavy mourners
Haste to Jordan's flood:

Some for sin their souls abasing;
Some to feed their eye with gazing;
    Some to search and try
With captious craft the shaggy preacher,
And themselves to teach the teacher;
    Some they know not why.

Comes the Rabbi, with a stately,
    Measured gravity;
With a solemn air, sedately
    Comes the Pharisee;
Wide his robe, and on the border
Sacred texts, in well-marched order
    Show his purpose plain,
With a nice and fenced existence,
Far to keep, at holy distance,
    Every touch profane.

Comes fat priest, and pontiff portly,
    With a bloated face;

Came Herodian, smooth and courtly,
    With a gay grimace.
Came the Essene from his station
Of secluded contemplation
    With mild gravity;
With an eye of twinkling keenness,
And a smile of cold sereneness,
    Came the Sadducee.

Comes the soldier firm and steady,
    Gallant, light, and gay,
With his quick hand ever ready
    For the rising fray.
Comes the usurer, dry and meagre,
Comes the publican, sharp and eager
    For great Cæsar's penny.
With a train of silken pages
Comes the rich man; with scant wages
    Come the burdened many.

What saith he, the wayside preacher,
　　To this motley crew?
Doth he come a cunning teacher
　　Of lore strange and new?
Hath he drawn without omission,
Point for point, a long confession,
　　To inform the brain?
Piled a proud word-architecture,
Fenced it round with fine conjecture,
　　And distinctions vain?

Hath he wove a girth to measure
　　God, a chain to bind
The Infinite, and mapped at leisure
　　The omniscient Mind?
Hath he trimmed an old theogony,
Cumbrous reared a new cosmogony,
　　To employ the schools?
Not with speculation vainest
Preacheth he;—with wisdom plainest
　　And with simplest rules.

Thus he speaks—'Repent! Repentance
Smooths Messiah's way;
'Tis an old and weighty sentence,
Weigh it well to-day.
Hast thou nursed a sin?—confess it;
Hast thou done a wrong?—redress it:
And, with just desire,
Ask no more than what is due thee:
Be content, when offered to thee,
With thy lawful hire.

Say not, with vain pride elated,
"God's own people we,
Tracing high a hoary-dated
Patriarch pedigree."
Peopled earth is thickly studded
With the children common-blooded,
Of the great I AM;
From the hard flint, at his pleasure,
God can raise up without measure
Sons to Abraham.

'Hear, whose barren trunk hath cumbered
    Now too long the ground,
Saith the Lord, your days are numbered;
    Hark! with crashing sound,
Falls the axe that fells the fruitless!
Toils he not with labour bootless
    Who now smites the tree.
He his winnowed wheat shall garner,
But like empty chaff the scorner
    Burn with fire shall he.'

Thus he preached to great and small men,
    Of the human right;
Like the blessed sun, on all men
    Shedding simple light.
O! wise are they who hear such preaching,
Not too high for common teaching
    In life's common ways;
Not with proud pretence ballooning,
Not with gay parade festooning,
    To catch the vulgar gaze.

Flap who will the air-borne pinion,
    Sweeping far and free;
Solid earth be my dominion,
    Baptist John, with thee!
In the plainest path of duty,
Stamping daily things with beauty,
    I with thee will tread;
Where thy warning finger pointed
I would follow, where the anointed
    Saviour lowly led!

Hymn to the Trinity.

I.

FIRST of all things primeval, hoar
Was THOUGHT, self-throned in glory,
Brooding with shaping might before
Each new Creation's story:
An unvoiced strength, a quiet power
Still pondering, still conceiving,
Unfathomed depth from hour to hour
With deathless virtue heaving;
Exhaustless, infinite to produce,
That in its gentle going
Weldeth the limbless and the loose
To reasoned beauty growing.
Hail, glorious THOUGHT, silent, sublime,
From thy divinest nature,

Sprang worlds on worlds from dateless time
First Father, First Creator,
Voice forth the hymn, loud pæans roll,
Ye thinking souls from pole to pole,
And round your centre gather!
Far peal his praise from jubilant throat,
Soul of all soul, thought of all thought,
The hidden God, the FATHER.

II.

SECOND of things the WORD forth-voiced
From the o'er-laden bosom
Of THOUGHT, that with itself rejoiced
And shook redundant blossom;
Swift-winged it flew, and journeying far
Like wave on wave it bounded,
And filled all space with vocal war
Of joy with joy confounded.
Prophetic WORD what wealth shall be
Of star-eyed expectation,

While Hope and Faith attend on thee,
Thou first bright incarnation
Of primal Thought divine! thou seed
With eager promise swelling,
And with strong pulse and measured speed
More stable growth compelling!
Voice ye the hymn, with pæans brim,
Your praise full-throated pour to him
From whom all Voices run!
Ye swelling hearts with high hopes stirred,
Hymn ye the prime prophetic WORD,
The published God, the SON.

III.

THIRD of all things forth marched at length
The DEED: soft breezy blowing
At first; anon to stout-limbed strength
Of compact body growing.
Informing SPIRIT! whence came the birth
Of fluent air and river

And fire with heaving heart, and Earth
That standeth stable ever.
The spangled web of vital strife
Thou weavest; Time thy story;
The world thy temple: human life
Thy battle-field of glory.
Soft shod, or with dread thunder pace
Thy sleepless march thou goest,
The thing that was stamped with thy trace
The thing to be, thou knowest.

Forth voice the hymn! from pole to pole
Him praise who breathed into your soul
The strength which ye inherit!
Each faithful heart that nobly strives,
Him praise, the life of all that lives
The all-working God, the SPIRIT.
First THOUGHT, first WORD, first DEED, these three.
Intelligential Trinity,
That was, and is, and is to be

One mystical Divinity!
Give ear, O Earth, and know the name,
The heart's deep awe commanding!
Fall on thy knees, O man, and blame
Thy brutish understanding!
Praise Him, the great, the Triune God,
Ye stable-rooted mountains!
Ye forests old, that darkly nod!
Ye full-mouthed gushing fountains!
Titanic tempests organ-roar,
Peal thou the strong Divinity;
Unsleeping wave that licks the shore
Sound thou the sleepless Trinity!
All million-throated things that be,
Voices of life's exuberant sea
With mingled hymns adore!
 The earthly and the heavenly host
To Father, Son, and Holy Ghost
 Sing glory evermore!

To the Divine Spirit.

SPIRIT that shaped the formless chaos,
Breath that stirred the sluggish deep,
When the primal crude creation
Started from its dateless sleep;
Spirit that heaved the granite mountains
From the central fiery wells,
Breath that drew the rolling rivers
From the welkin's dewy cells,
Spirit of motion,
Earth and ocean
Moulding into various life,
Within, without us,
And round about us
Weaving all in friendly strife:

Come, O come, thou heavenly guest,
Shape a new world within my breast!

Spirit that taught the holy fathers
  Wandering through the desert drear,
To know and feel, through myriad marchings,
  One eternal presence near.
Breath that touched the Hebrew prophets'
  Lips with words of wingèd fire,
Through the dubious gloom of ages,
  Kindling hope and high desire:
        Spirit revealing
        To pure feeling,
  In the inward parts of man,
        Fitful-shining
        Dim-divining
  Vast foreshadowings of Thy plan;
Come, O come, thou prophet guest,
Watch and wait within my breast

Spirit, that o'er Thine own Messiah
  Hovered like a brooding dove,
When Earth's haughty lords He conquered,
  By the peaceful march of love.
Breath that hushed loud-vaunting Cæsars,
  And in triumph yoked to Thee
Iron Rome, and savage Scythia,
  Bonded brethren and the free.
      Spirit of union,
      And communion
  Of devoted heart with heart,
      Pure and holy
      Sure and slowly
  Working out thy boastless part:
Come, thou calmly-conquering guest,
Rule and reign within my breast!

Spirit that, when free-thoughted Europe
  With the triple-crowned despot strove,

In the gusty Saxon's spirit
  Thy soul-stirring music wove;
Then when pride's piled architecture
  At a poor monk's truthful word
Crashing fell, and thrones were shaken
  At the whisper of the Lord.
      Spirit deep-lurking,
      Secret-working
  Weaver of strange circumstance,
      All whose doing
      Is rise or ruin
  Named by shallow mortals chance;
Come, let fruitful deeds attest
Thy plastic virtue, in my breast!

Spirit, that sway'st the will of mortals,
  Every wish, and every hope,
Shaping to Thy forethought purpose
  All their striving, all their scope.

Central tide that heavest onward
  Wave and wavelet, surge and spray,
Making wrath of man to praise Thee,
  And his pride to pave Thy way:
    Spirit that workest.
    Where Thou lurkest,
  Death from life, and day from night,
    Peace from warring,
    And from jarring,
  Songs of triumph and delight;
Come, O come, Thou heavenly guest,
Work all Thy will within my breast!

To the Saviour.

O THOU, by men the Saviour vaunted,
Beyond all mighty names that were,
    Invoked and chanted!
Supreme above all strifes that stir
This troublous zone, as high in Heaven,
Vaulting the dark clouds thunder-riven,
Hangs poised the dome of lucid day
    Serenely stable;
If thou, as when our fleshly frame
To thy pure spirit gave place and name,
    To save art able,
Me, thy poor brother—for I may call
Thee with what name thou gav'st to all—

From lawless thoughts, and heartless deeds,
And from the strife of harnessed creeds
Save—O my Saviour!

Proud temples to the mighty Saviour
The boastful sons of men have raised
With fair behaviour,
With laboured litanies have praised
A Saviour's name. Even so of old,
Who tricked the prophets' tombs with gold
Thy living prophet's person nailed
With crucifixion;
And we with worship of thy name
Do cheat ourselves of Thee, nor blame
The shallow fiction.
Where love is cold, and loose lust reigns,
And pride ramps insolent in the veins,
Where earthy souls heap earthy dross,
And deedless fear shrinks back from loss,
Art thou the Saviour?

By the green waves of ancient Constance,
Convened in Christ the Saviour's name,
With pomp and instance,
The scarlet-hatted churchmen came.
And kings and kaisers with the cowl
Were leagued that day, by fair or foul
To smite a just man's truthful front
With sore infliction.
Erect up stood that pale-faced man,
And mildly met the purple ban
With contradiction.
Hate, Pride, and Fear, with axe and rod,
And pious phrase, assumed the god;
A solemn sentence then did frame,
And burnt the just man in the name
Of Christ the Saviour.

Even so; and this was then religion!
But look within, false heart, and read
In that home region

What germs of strange delusion breed;
What snake, there lurking 'neath the flower,
Waits but the tempter's suasive hour,
When he in some new guise shall show
    The dear temptation:
O! then, whom men the Saviour call,
From stumbling save and sudden fall,
    And sheer prostration!
From loveless will and untamed thought,
From vain desire and fancies naught,
From the deaf ear that hears no call,
From pride that pioneers a fall,
    Be thou my Saviour!

Ode to Christian Love.

BARDS sing of love, and songsters of the wood
Thrill with strong love the leafy solitude,
When Spring walks forth in power;
Harsh natures melt; the cold and flinty glow;
And close-locked hearts expand in flowery show,
When passion's fervid hour
Usurps them. But not passion's subtlest flame,
That stirs the gentle bard's nice-tempered frame,
Nor mated warbler's lay,
That rolls in luscious streams through leafy wood,
Nor that soft thrill which melts each harshest mood,
Can match thy queenly sway,

Strong Christian love! Thou with no partial fire
Dost stir the breast; no fitful wild desire
Tosses the soul serene,
Where thy calm ardour glows; but, like the ray
Of that great Light, which rules the constant day,
With life-diffusing sheen,
So thou, bright-seated on the central throne
Of holy hearts dost shine. Thus thou wert known
To faithful men of yore;
Thee Moses knew, when, through the desert track,
He led the unstable stiff-necked army back
From Egypt's servile shore,
To their ancestral hills. The preacher Paul
Owned thy intensest sway, when to the call
Of God he oped his ear,
And strong by thee, like feeble withes, he snapt
The bonds of custom, and, in transport rapt,
Saw heavenly visions clear.
Then o'er the Earth with wingèd tread he flew,
And East and West his burning message knew;
The dull barbarian's home

With rapture hailed his heart-reviving note ;
His word with quick regeneration smote
        The tainted heart of Rome,
And subtle Greece with her light-vagrant eye
Screens from reproof her fair idolatry,
        Unweeded fancy's flower
Vainly. No more glib Athens may dispute,
And Corinth's tinkling harlotry is mute.
        When Paul, with earnest power,
Proclaims the cross.—O Thou inspiring God,
Whose shaping virtue doth inform the clod,
        With warm life teeming ever ;
With some pure spark of thine all-conquering love
Touch Thou my heart, that all my ways may prove
        Thy strength, which faileth never !

Night.

'Ιερὰ Νύξ.—HOMER.

HOLY NIGHT! in silence
From thy starry throne
Swaying, thee I worship,
Silent and alone.

Holy Night! how calmly
Sails the mellow moon
Through the deep blue welkin,
Fairer than the noon.

Mellow Moon! how gently
Through the voiceless night,
O'er the sleeping waters,
Streams thy silver light.

Holy Night! how lovely
  Shoot, with sudden birth,
Hosts of shimmering arrows
  From the lambent north.

Holy Night! thou reignest
  Solemn, still, serene;
Hushed the tribes of mortals
  Bow before their queen.

Now the battling voices
  Of the babbling throng
Cease; and thou may'st listen,
  As it treads along,

To the steps of Godhead
  Beating march of Time,
Slowly, surely, wisely,
  Beautiful, sublime;

Beating thought and feeling,
  Beating vital power
In renewed creation's
  Pulse, from hour to hour.

Holy Night! devoutly
  While I worship thee,
Babbling Folly's echo
  Dies away from me.

A Sabbath Meditation.

THE Sabbath bells are travelling o'er the hill;
The gentle breeze across the fresh-reaped fields
Blows fitful; scarcely, on the broad smooth bay,
With full white-gleaming sail, the slow ship moves;
Thin float the clouds; serene the mountain stands;
And all the plain in hallowed beauty lies.
God of the Sabbath, on thy holy day
'Tis meet to praise Thee! In the high-domed fane,
Glorious with all the legendary pomp
Of pictured saints, where skilful singers swell
The curious chant, or on the lonely hill,
Where, on grey cliff and purple heather, shines
The shadowless sun at noon, Thou hear'st alike.
Vainly the narrow wit of narrow men

Within the walls which priestly lips have blest,
In the fixed phrases of a formal creed,
Would crib thy presence; Thou art more than all
The shrines that hold Thee; and our wisest creeds
Are but the lispings of a prattling child,
To spell the Infinite. Kings have drawn the sword,
Lawyers have wrangled, to declare thy being;
And convocations of high-mitred men
The foaming vials of sacerdotal wrath
Outpoured, and, with tempestuous proud conceit,
Shook the vast world about a phrase to name Thee,
In vain. Thou, like the thin impassive air,
Dost cheat the grasp of subtlest-thoughted sage;
And half our high theology is but
The shadow, which man's poor and clouded ken
Hath cast across thy brightness. I would sing
Thy praise with humble heart, and, like the lyre
Wind-swept, the comings of thy breath would wait
To wake my rapture. Lift up your heads, ye hills,
And nod His praise, ye sharp far-stretching lines

Of crags storm-shattered, and ye jagged peaks
Sky-cleaving! you His mighty power upshot
From the red ocean of His nethermost fire,
In primal ages: there inform ye lay,
In seething lakes, your molten masses huge,
In turbid waves, with inorganic roll,
Far-heaving through the dark abysmal space
Chaotic; thence His word creative hove
Your marshalled ridges; rank on rank ye rose,
Granite and gneiss, and every ordered kind
That careful science counts; the giant frame
Of this fair world, of peace-enfolden vales
Storm-fronting fence, and bulwark ever sure.
Ye mountain torrents, with far-sweeping foam,
Ye leaping cataracts, and deep-swirling pools,
Ye streams with the full-gathered grandeur rolling
Of countless rills, from huge far-sundered Alps,
Ye waters, with your thousand voices, praise
The mighty Lord! He of your sleepless floods
Is the unsleeping soul. All motion comes

From Him. Thou Ocean, with thy living belt
Girdling the Earth, whether serene, as now,
Thou liest, licking with an innocent ripple
The feet o' the green-throned isles, or, like a spurred
And furious charger, wild from coast to coast
Drivest far-sounding—thou, in all thy changes,
Art full of God; yea, all thy works, O Lord,
Are full of Thee! and who is dull to these
Shall from the teaching of the schools come back
With beggarly blindness. He shall mount in vain
His telescope, to spy Thee in the clouds,
Who in green herb and starry flower, beneath
His vagrant foot, hath failed to see and love
Thy manifest beauty. O make clear my sense,
Thou great Revealer, to the grand array
Of open mysteries that encompass round
Our daily walk with Godhead, that no vain
And wordy fool may cheat my facile ear
With echoed vollies of man's crude conceit,
Misnamed God's thunder! From Thyself direct

Thy secret comes to all, whom Thou shalt deem
Worthy to find it. Councils, doctors, priests,
Are but the signs that point us to the spring
Whence flow thy living waters; and, alas!
Too oft with wavering, or with cowardly hand
Back-turned, they point. Teach Thou my stablished
soul
To seek Thy teaching, Lord, and trust in Thee.

The generations of uncounted men
Have hymned Thy praises, Lord. Their stammering
tongues
With strange crude doctrine magnify the power
Of Him, whose vastness they were fain to grasp,
But could not. Even the folly of the fool
Shall praise Thee, Lord. Thou hast a place for all.
The wicked and the weak are but the steps,
Whereon the wise shall mount, to see Thy face;
And mighty churches, and high-vaunted faiths,

Are but the schools, wherein thy centuries train
The infant peoples to the manly reach
Of pure devotion; and most wise are they,
Who hear one hymn of varied truth through all
The harmonious discord of strange witnesses,
Prophets and martyrs, priests, and meek-eyed saints,
And rapt diviners, with imperfect tongue,
Babbling thy praises. Egypt's brutish gods,
Dog-faced, hawk-headed, crocodile, and cat,
Snake-eating ibis, and the spotted bull,
Not without apt significance did type
Thy severed functions to a sense-bound race.
In sea and sky, green tree, and flowing stream,
In flying bird, and creeping beast, they found
Pictorial speech, and speaking signs of what
They crudely guessed of Thee. To clearer Greeks
Stout Briareus, celestial Titans strong,
And supreme Jove, with weight of thunderous locks,
Throned like a king, and sceptre in his hand,
And ministrant eagle, spake thy mighty power

With awful grace. Each seized a part of Thee,
And, with a fond assurance, deemed to hold
Thy whole Infinity in earthly bonds
For human needs. Nor less the Christian priest
Portentous erred, when with rash hand he clutched
The awful Triune symbol, and defined
The immeasurable Majesty Supreme
With curious phrase and scientific rule,
And with the thorns of wiry logic fenced
Thy bristling name, from touch of thought profane;
Then, from a throne high-seated, and girt round
With triple-tiered presumption, grasped thy bolt,
Sported thy thunder, and with thy best friends
Filled a far-dreaded Hell, that he might seem
A god on Earth, whom awe-struck, grovelling men
Might see, and feel, and handle. The pale monk,
Wasting his flesh within a cold damp cell,
And straining his dull vision, till he saw
God's features, in the dim putrescent light
Of his own sick imaginings—this man caught

A glimpse of Thee, and, with such fiery haste
Did hold Thee, and with prostrate worship hug,
That nevermore his head he dared to lift
Erect, and with proud-sweeping glance survey
The riches of thy wide luxuriant world,
Man's privilege.—On so nice a pivot turns
True wisdom; here an inch, or there, we swerve
From the just balance; by too much we sin,
And half our errors are but truths unpruned.

The errors of Thy creatures praise Thee, Lord.
Not they who err are damned; but who, being wrong,
In obdurate persistency to err
Refuse all bettering. Hope for such is none.
Hope lives for all, who flounder boldly on
Through quaggy bogs, till firmer footing found
Gives glorious prospect. One Deceiver haunts
The hearts of faithless men; his name is FEAR.
O Thou, who ridest glorious through the skies,

In thunder or in sunshine strong the same,
The Almighty builder of this fair machine,
Whose beauty blinds star-eyed philosophy,
Whose vastness makes our staggered thinking pant
For utterance vainly—Father of all Power,
Eternal Fount of liberty and life,
Free, measureless, unspent—if e'er my voice
Rose to thy throne, in reverent truthful prayer,
Slay me this demon, yellow Fear, that maims
The arm of enterprise, nips the bud of hope,
And freezes the great ocean of our life,
That should run riot in the praise of Thee,
With wave on wave of proud high-venturing deeds.
O may this Sabbath, with its gentle dews
Shed by thy Spirit on my chastened soul,
Restore my blighted bud of thought, and lift
This low-crushed life into a mighty tree,
Branchy, and blooming with fair summer fruits
Exuberant-clustered !—May all Sabbaths be
A ripe and mellow season to my heart,

Lovely as golden autumn's purple eve,
Genial as sleep, whence the tired limb refreshed
Leaps to new action, and appointed toil,
With steady hope, sure faith, and sober joy.

The Sea.

WHAT dost thou say,
Thou old grey sea,
Thou broad briny water
To me?
With thy ripple and thy plash,
And thy waves as they lash
The old grey rocks on the shore?
With thy tempests as they roar,
And thy crested billows hoar,
And thy tide evermore,
Fresh and free;
With thy floods as they come,
And thy voice never dumb,
What thought art thou speaking to me?

What thing should I say
On this bright summer day,
Thou strange human dreamer, to thee?
One wonder the same
All things do proclaim
In the sky, and the land, and the sea;
'Tis the unsleeping force
Of a God in his course,
Whose life is the law of the whole,
As he breathes out his power
In the pulse of the hour,
And the march of the years as they roll;
You may measure his ways
In the weeks and the days,
And the stars as they wheel round the pole,
But no finger is thine
To touch the divine
All-plastic, all-permeant soul,
As it shapes and it moulds,
And its virtue unfolds,

In the garden of things as they grow,
    And flings forth the tide
    Of its strength far and wide,
In wonders above and below.

    Thou huge-heaving sea
    That art speaking to me
Of the power and the pride of a God,
    I would travel like thee
    With force fresh and free
Through the breadth of my human abode,
    Never languid and low,
    But with bountiful flow,
Of thoughts that are kindred to God;
    Ever surging and streaming,
    Ever beaming and gleaming,
Like the lights as they shift on thy glass,
    Ever swelling and heaving,
    And largely receiving
The beauty of things as they pass.

Thou broad-billowed sea
Never sundered from thee
May I wander the welkin below;
May the plash and the roar
Of thy waves on the shore
Beat the march to my feet as they go;
Ever strong, ever free,
When the breath of the sea
Like the fan of an angel I know;
Ever rising with power,
To the call of the hour,
Like the swell of thy tides as they flow.

Lift up your Hymns, all Men.

A SONG OF PRAISE FOR BRITISH WORKMEN.

(*Tune*—Old 148th Psalm.)

LIFT up your hymns, all men
Who scan with lordly eye,
And mete with kingly ken
The starry-peopled sky;
Praise ye the God
Who bade ye tread,
With lofty head,
Earth's lowly sod!

Time was when ye were not;
Through lightless depths forlorn
The Eternal Father shot
His ray, and ye were born.

Even Him praise ye,
Whose quickening light
Redeems from night
All things that be.

How wondrous each fair form
Of life that swarms on earth,
Light fowl and ringèd worm,
And stout four-footed birth!
But, lord of all,
High-fronted man
To crown His plan
God's voice did call.

Look forth, O man, and know
Thy glorious mission given
To rule the earth below
With wisdom lent from heaven.
To His command
Obedience bring

Who made thee king
Of sea and land!

From ice-bound pole to pole,
From sunny zone to zone,
March forth with venturous soul
And claim the world thine own;
And praise Him ever
Who bade thy hand
Rule sea and land
With proud endeavour!

The granite boulders vast
Split with thy mastering wedge,
The gusty-driving blast
Rein on the billow's edge;
And understand
By what high claim
Thy wit doth tame
Both sea and land.

With cylinder and beam
  And fine-conducting skill,
Torture the straitened steam
  To work thy reasoned will;
    And understand
    How Godlike Mind
    The power doth bind
    Of sea and land!

With bolt and bar and clamp
  And strong-subduing fire,
And chymick virtue stamp
  All things to thy desire;
    For God in heaven
    Such shaping skill
    To man's wise will
    Hath surely given.

Pile high th' embattled tower,
  And where the huge seas roll

With arms of Titan power
Fling forth the mighty mole,
Whose strength doth save
Brave hearts from scaith
Of yawning Death
And yeasty grave!

Stretch forth the pendant bridge,
'Cross the broad-breasted tide,
And round the steep-faced ridge
On smoking chariot ride,
Even as a bird
Well-used to soar
His plumy oar
Hath lightly stirred.

And let thy lordly hest,
And thy heart's hot desire
Be sped to East and West
Swift through the thrilling wire,

O'er earth and sea,
Which God the Lord
Did well accord
A stage for thee!

Lift up thy head, O man,
And walk rejoicing forth,
To sway with sweatful plan
The stubborn-breasted earth.
Thus shalt thou be
Liegeman of God,
Trèading earth's sod
Erect and free!

The School of Jesus.

COME unto me, who live in cumbrous splendour,
'Neath Fashion's despot rule,
And to meek Wisdom's kindly sway surrender
Your hearts in Jesus' school.

No pomp is here of gold and purple flaunting,
No banners proudly spread,
No trumpet's blare, no victor's cruel vaunting,
No field bestrewn with dead.

No high-set throne with glittering throngs attendant,
No loud far-sounded name,
Sceptre or sword, or robe with gems resplendent,
To blaze His peaceful fame.

But contemplation chaste serenely brooding
With clear unclouded face,
High thought that scorns all baser cares intruding
Into God's holy place.

And mighty love embracing all things human
In one all-fathering name,
Stamping God's seal on trivial things and common,
With consecrated aim.

The godlike front, the mouth of bold confession,
The conquering glance of truth,.
The hand that works with the sure slow progression
Of unrecorded growth.

The breath that blows with quickening vans victorious
O'er realms of thought sublime,
Making our life a golden harvest glorious,
Reaped from the fields of time.

In vain, in vain, to rouse your languid leisure,
Ye waste ancestral stores,
Starring with gold your wide-domed halls of pleasure,
And treading pictured floors.

In vain from show to show ye drive unsated,
And sights of gay surprise;
The soul's high hunger rests all unabated
From gaze of wondering eyes.

Stir the deep wells of life that flow within you,
Touched by God's genial hand,
And let the chastened sure ambition win you
To serve His high command,

And cast aside the costly cumbrous splendour
Of Fashion's despot rule,
And to meek Wisdom's kindly sway surrender
Your hearts in Jesus' school.

Prayer for Direction.

LORD of might, and Lord of glory,
On my knees I bow before Thee,
With my whole heart I adore Thee,
Great Lord!
Listen to my cry, O Lord!

Passions proud and fierce have ruled me,
Fancies light and vain have fooled me,
But Thy training stern hath schooled me;
Now, Lord,
Take me for Thy child, O Lord!

Groping dim, and bending lowly,
Mortal vision catcheth slowly
Glimpses of the pure and holy;
        Now, Lord,
Open Thou mine eyes, O Lord!

Not with lofty thoughts far-reaching,
Not with blasts of mightful preaching,
But with heart that waits Thy teaching,
        Good Lord,
Let me learn from Thee, O Lord!

Not where dazzling glories win us,
Not where sounding plaudits din us,
But Thy kingdom is within us,
        There, Lord,
Let Thy truth teach me, O Lord!

In the deed that no man knoweth,
Where no praiseful trumpet bloweth,
Where he may not reap who soweth,
        There, Lord,
Let my heart serve Thee, O Lord!

In the work that no gold payeth,
Where he speedeth best who prayeth,
Doeth most who little sayeth,
        There, Lord,
Let me work Thy will, O Lord!

In His name who, meek and lowly,
Died to make poor sinners holy,
Stumbling oft, and creeping slowly,
        Great Lord,
Guide me by Thy truth, O Lord!

The God of Glee

Aber die Götter lieben der Menschen
Weitverbreitete gute Geschlechter.

GOETHE.

IF a mortal man might sing
Theme above all mortal wing;
If the creatures of the clay
With the name of God might play;
If the moulded breath might tell
All that stirs the soul's deep well,
I would sing a song of glee,
Father of all songs, to Thee!

Thou art not the awful thing,
Iron ruler, despot king,
Harsh, revengeful, stern, severe,
Child of terror, birth of fear:

Thou art nothing like to Him,
Ghost of sickly dreamer's whim;
If I sing a song to Thee,
It shall be a song of glee.

Fools may rant, and fools may rave,
Loudly damn, and loudly save,
With a solemn sounding swell,
Sweeping honest souls to hell,
With church-blasts of mimic thunder
Turning every over under;
Thou from wrath of man art free,
God of gladness, God of glee!

What Thou art no tongue may say;
I remember I am clay;
Scarcely knowing brother man,
Shall I venture God to scan?

From within and from without
Full of dream, and full of doubt,
Feeling only lent from Thee,
This glad Being, God of glee!

Shall I set Thee on a throne
Ruling solemnly alone?
Shall I dress Thee in strange glory?
Grandly chant Thy epic story?
Shall I lodge Thee in the tomb,
There to lighten up my gloom?
Shalt Thou sleep in death with me,
God of gladness, God of glee?

Shall my wit be Thine inspector?
Shall my knife be Thy dissector?
Shall I perch Thee on a steeple,
To feed the gaze of gaping people?

Shall I show Thee round and round,
Here explain, and there expound?
In a cold creed prison Thee,
God of gladness, God of glee?

Shalt Thou be my sworn director,
Patroniser, and protector?
Shall I stamp with Thy great seal
All I think, and all I feel?
Shalt Thou be a horse to ride
For the pranks of human pride?
And shall strife be born of Thee,
God of gladness, God of glee?

Shalt Thou hug me in Thy breast,
Fledgling of no human nest?
Shall I be the one pet-lamb
Of the terrible I AM?

I the called and the elect,
Thou Jehovah of a sect?
Bastards all, save only me,
Thou, *my* Father, God of glee?

O! it is a hard assay
For the reach of human clay,
And yet every fool will mount
Thee to number, Thee to count,
With a plummet and a square
Meting out the pathless air;
Teach me how to think of Thee,
God of gladness, God of glee!

If my tongue must lisp its lay,
I will speak what best I may:
I will say, Thou art a Soul,
Weaving wisely through the whole;

I will say Thou art a Power
Working good from hour to hour,
I will say Thou art to me
Light and Life, and Love and Glee.

Thou art each, and Thou art all
In Creation's living Hall,
Every breathing shape of beauty,
Every solemn voice of duty!
Every high and holy mood,
All that 's great, and all that 's good,
All is Echo sent from Thee,
God of gladness, God of glee!

Laws of Nature.

THE fool hath in his heart declared,—by laws
Since time began,
Blind and without intelligential cause,
Or reasoned plan,
All things are ruled. I from this lore dissent,
With sorrowful shame
That reasoning men such witless wit should vent
In reason's name.
O Thou that o'er this lovely world hast spread
Thy jocund light,
Weaving with flowers beneath, and stars o'erhead
This tissue bright
Of living powers, clear Thou my sense, that I
May ever find

In all the marshalled pomp of earth and sky
　　　　The marshalling mind!
Laws are not powers; nor can the well-timed courses
　　　　Of earths and moons
Ring to the stroke of blind unthinking forces
　　　　Their jarless tunes.
Wiser were they who in the flaming vault
　　　　The circling sun
Beheld, and in his ray, with splendid fault,
　　　　Worshipped the one
Eye of the universe that seeth all,
　　　　And shapeth sight
In man and moth through curious visual ball
　　　　With fine delight.
O blessed beam, on whose refreshful might
　　　　Profusely shed
Six times ten years, with ever young delight,
　　　　Mine eye hath fed,
Still let me love thee, and with wonder new,
　　　　By flood and field,

Worship the fair, and consecrate the true
          By thee revealed!
And loving thee, beyond thee love that first
          Father of Lights
From whom the ray vivific marvellous burst,
          Might of all mights,
Whose thought is order, and whose will is law.
          That man is wise
Who worships God wide-eyed, with cheerful awe
          And chaste surprise.

What is Nature.

WHAT thing is Nature? Well, I don't
Assume to make a clatter,
Like Hegel, Hamilton, and Comte,
Concerning mind and matter.

Yet I have had my thoughts at times;
And, since you ask the question,
I'll tell you what I think in rhymes
That won't hurt your digestion.

Nature is growth, a coming forth
Into new fashion ever,
Of that whose substance knows no birth,
Whose virtue dieth never.

What Substance?—that which to define
  My gasping reason smothers;
But what is best I call divine,
  And worship God with others.

You're a materialist? Not at all;
  If I should seek to find
The best name for what BEST I call,
  I'd rather call it MIND.

And Mind is one; and what we call
  The Many is but one,
As million rays shoot from the ball
  Of th' light-evolving Sun.

But not to dogmas I incline,
  And think me not unwise
Who fear and love, but not define,
  The Power that shapes the skies.

And you, Sir Doctor, are a fool,
  With logical appliance,
That would take God into your school,
  And teach Him terms of science;

And talk of Nature, God, and Man
  With technic demonstration,
As if yourself had sketched the plan
  Of the boundless, vast Creation;

And dress mean thoughts in phrases grand,
  And prove, with solemn clatter,
That you have got, in your clumsy hand,
  Two things called Mind and Matter.

Go to! You know nor this, nor that;
  Man has no measuring rod
For Nature, Force, and Law, and what
  The wisest men call GOD.

For law, and life, and all the course
  Of lovely-shifting Nature,
Are but the play of one wise Force,
  Which Moses called Creator.

Think on your knees: 'tis better so
  Than without wings to soar;
What blinking Reason strains to know
  We find when we adore.

All things are full of God.

Ο Θαλῆς τὸν κόσμον ἔμψυχον ὑπεστήσατο καὶ δαιμόνων πλήρη.

DIOG. LAERT.

I.

ALL things are full of God. Thus spoke
  Wise Thales in the days
When subtle Greece to thought awoke
  And soared in lofty ways.
And now what wisdom have we more?
  No sage divining-rod
Hath taught than this a deeper lore,
  ALL THINGS ARE FULL OF GOD.

II.

The Light that gloweth in the sky
And shimmers in the sea,
That quivers in the painted fly
And gems the pictured lea,
The million hues of Heaven above
And Earth below are one,
And every lightful eye doth love
The primal light, the Sun.

III.

Even so, all vital virtue flows
From life's first fountain, God;
And he who feels, and he who knows,
Doth feel and know from God.
As fishes swim in briny sea,
As fowl do float in air,
From Thy embrace we cannot flee;
We breathe, and Thou art there.

IV.

Go, take thy glass, astronomer,
  And all the girth survey
Of sphere harmonious linked to sphere,
  In endless bright array.
All that far-reaching Science there
  Can measure with her rod,
All powers, all laws, are but the fair
  Embodied thoughts of God.

V.

And if there be who of blind laws
  And soulless forces talk,
Who feed vain doubts with fancied flaws,
  With these I will not walk.
But as a child to father clings,
  Or flower to sapful sod,
The living well within me springs
  Of all great thoughts from God.

VI.

O Thou, who didst the heart inspire
  Of Thales and his peers,
And touched the prophet-lips with fire
  Of holy Hebrew seers,
Teach Thou in great and small my will
  To own Thy sovereign rod,
Holding this faith firm-rooted still,
  ALL THINGS ARE FULL OF GOD.

Prayer.

'WHY wilt thou pray? why storm with cries
His ear who rides the thundering skies,
    And passes wrathful by?
His laws stand firm; He may not hear;
Thy life, thy death, in His career
Are but as steps. He will not hear
    Though thou shalt loudly cry.'

Most like, most like! yet the soft tear
Fresh dropt upon the senseless bier
    Hath virtue—nor that small.
The sod why dost thou strew with flowers?
The dead man walks not in thy bowers,
He will not rise to sorrow's showers,
    Nor feel when soft flowers fall;

And yet thou weep'st. Much more may'st thou
Pay to the living God thy vow,
    And pour the heart-felt prayer.
Deft Logic is but Reason's tool,
Reason a child in Nature's school;
We may not joy nor grieve by rule,
    Nor syllogise a prayer.

Sabbath Hymn on the Mountains.

PRAISE ye the Lord!
Not in the temple of shapeliest mould,
Polished with marble and gleaming with gold,
Piled upon pillars of slenderest grace,
But here in the blue sky's luminous face
Praise ye the Lord!

Praise ye the Lord!
Not where the organ's melodious wave
Dies 'neath the rafters that narrow the nave,
But here with the free wind's wandering sweep,
Here with the billow that booms from the deep,
Praise ye the Lord!

Praise ye the Lord!
Not where the pale-faced multitudes meet
In the sweltering lane, and the dun-visaged street,
But here where bright ocean, thick sown with green isles,
Feeds the glad eye with a harvest of smiles,
Praise ye the Lord!

Praise ye the Lord!
Here where the strength of the old granite Ben
Towers o'er the greenswarded grace of the glen,
Where the birch flings its fragrance abroad on the hill,
And the bee o'er the heather-bloom wanders at will,
Praise ye the Lord!

Praise ye the Lord!
Here where the loch, the dark mountain's fair daughter,
Down the red scaur flings the white-streaming water,

Leaping and tossing and swirling for ever
Down to the bed of the smooth-rolling river,
Praise ye the Lord!

Praise ye the Lord!
Not where the voice of a preacher instructs you,
Not where the hand of a mortal conducts you,
But where the bright welkin in scripture of glory
Blazons Creation's miraculous story,
Praise ye the Lord!

Praise ye the Lord!
The wind and the welkin, the sun and the river,
Weaving a tissue of wonders for ever;
The mead and the mountain, the flower and the tree,
What is their pomp but a vision of Thee,
Wonderful Lord?

Praise ye the Lord!
Not in the square-hewn, many-tiered pile,
Not in the long-drawn, dim-shadowed aisle,
But where the vast world, with age never hoary,
Flashes His brightness and thunders His glory,
Praise ye the Lord!

Trimurti.

TRIMURTI, Trimurti,
Mock not the name;
Think and know
Before thou blame!

Brother, believe me, I respect thy creed,
And in mine inmost shrine of reverence bow
Before the men of strong firm-jointed thought
Who framed, and with their hearts' warm life-blood
signed
That paper—thy confession; but to fling
Damnation round against all other creeds,
And plant myself, draped in most fine conceit,
And laced in Orthodoxy all compact,

A model for all forms of thought that be,
Is not my fashion, and should not be yours.
Thy sun-tanned brother in the glowing East,
Where sacred Ganga rolls his ample flood,
Bends not the knee to senseless blocks and beasts
But to a SPIRIT: and his huge gilded idols
Are but the clumsier spelling of a name
Which no man spells completely: he believes
In his own way, what you believe in yours.
Him, too, the power of Universal God
Hath touched: he, too, discerns the Soul that stirs
The heaving clod: the mystery of life
He probes: and in the battling din of things
That frets the feeble ear, he seeks and finds
A harmony that tunes the dissonant strife
To sweetest music. If in the sober West
High thought, and awful power of Hebrew faith
Hath taught thee much, and seemed to teach thee
more,
Love more thy brother from thy larger breast.

Trimurti, Trimurti,
  Despise not the name;
Think and know
  Before thou blame!

Look upon the face of Nature
  In the flush of June;
BRAHMA is the great Creator,
  Life is Brahma's boon.
Dost thou hear the zephyr blowing?
  That is Brahma's breath,
Vital breath, live virtue showing
  'Neath the ribs of death.
Dost thou see the fountain flowing?
  That is Bramah's blood,
Lucid blood—the same is glowing
  In the purpling bud.
Brahma's Eyes look forth divining
  From the welkin's brow,
Full bright eyes—the same are shining
  In the sacred cow.

Air, and Fire, and running River,
  And the procreant clod,
Are but faces changing ever
  Of one changeless God.
When thy wingèd thought ascendeth
  Where high thoughts are free,
This is Brahma when he lendeth
  Half the God to thee.
Brahma is the great Creator,
  Life a mystic drama;
Heaven, and Earth, and living Nature
  Are but masks of Brahma.

Trimurti, Trimurti,
  Mock not the name;
Think and know
  Before thou blame!

Awful SIVA dost thou know?
Awful SIVA I will show.

SIVA, RUDRA, MAHADEVA,
  One with many a shifting name,
BHIMA, UGRA, PASAPATI,
  Never like, but still the same!
Earth is dumb with awe and wonder,
  When it sees dark Siva come;
Nations pale to hear the thunder
  Of his fateful-pealing drum.
When he rides with serpents belted,
  Pearled with skulls about his neck,
Rocks beneath his tread are melted,
  Mighty empires fall in wreck;
    In the flood and in the flame
    Terrible is Siva's name.
Dost thou see yon tiny boat
  Cradled in the shimmering ocean?
Summer clouds that lightly float
  Sail not with a gentler motion.
Canst thou hear the merry notes
  From the jocund sailors pealing,

Careless joy from clamorous throats,
  Floods of free ebullient feeling?
Suddenly there comes a blast;
  With short fits of gusty terror
Quakes the air: night travels fast;
  Darkly glooms the briny horror.
Where is now that gamesome boat?
  Where the crew with wild joy swelling?
Seek them in dark ocean's throat,
  In the mute sea-monster's dwelling.
Mighty SIVA hath prevailed:
  On the tempest's wings of madness
Riding, harsh and iron-mailed,
  He hath crushed all joy and gladness.
Many mothers weep to-day,
  Many brides will weep to-morrow,—
SIVA comes, and leaves his way
  Washed with blood, and paved with sorrow;
SIVA comes: his power adore;
  Wrathful treads the great Destroyer,

Death, his servant, walks before,
  Teeming Life is his employer.
Famine, Fever, Flood, and Flame,
  Murder and the Grave,
Rulé by mighty Siva's name;
  None from him can save.
Worship SIVA: when he glares
  With his three red eyes of Ruin,
When his smoking breath prepares
  Three-pronged bolts for thy undoing.
Bend the knee beneath his dart,
  Huts may stand, while towers shall crumble;
Crushing low the proud in heart,
  Siva oft hath spared the humble.

Trimurti, Trimurti,
  Mock not the name;
Search and know
  Before thou blame!

All-pervading, all-informing,
  Heart of heat within the cold,
Widely-working, richly-warming,
  VISHNU loves to melt and mould.
Though SIVA hath passed in the stormy blast,
  And, like a crimson streamer,
Hath swept the sky, Vishnu is nigh;
  Earth looks for her Redeemer.
Six months and a day grim Winter's sway
  May last, but not for ever;
The grass shall grow, and the bud shall blow,
  When Vishnu unbinds the river.
Long is the sleep that nations sleep;
  Bleak centuries they lie
Confounded, or convulsive creep
  In wriggling agony.
But still the hidden life they keep;
  Regeneration lurks;
A heaving God shall stir the clod
  Where mighty Vishnu works.

Deserts, when they feel his tread,
  Wave with leafy surges,
Yama from their bony bed
  His refleshed ghosts disgorges.
Wouldst thou grasp him? that is hard,
  With three giant paces
Who hath strode the blue girth barred
  To worms in mortal cases.
Wouldst thou know him? that is hard;
  He holds no certain shape;
Soldier, prophet, priest, or bard,
  Fish, or boar, or ape,
All and each are Vishnu's faces;
  But the wise behind
Each rude mask discern the traces
  Of the Saviour-Mind.
They shall know him who believe
  That through his incarnation,
Faithful hearts and hands achieve
  The world's regeneration.

They shall leave the half-burnt stake,
  And the half-ploughed furrow,
And their portion they shall make
  With Vishnu's joy and sorrow.
They with him shall toil and travel,
  For him fight and bleed:
For Vishnu, though Hell's legions cavil,
  In the end shall speed.
With an iron-pointed will,
  A steady-glowing fervour,
Vanquished, they are victors still
  Through Vishnu the PRESERVER.
Small as a seed that 's cast on Earth
  Vishnu's power is planted,
Wide as ocean's swelling girth
  Vishnu's growth is vaunted.
Like a beggar first he shows,
  And great and small ignore him;
Anon in regal pomp he goes,
  And monarchs bend before him.

Where he comes each palsied heart
  Beats with quick emotion,
Peoples into being start,
  And Earth upheaves like Ocean.
Rags of false fair Pride are torn,
  Truth's bright blazon flutters,
Tears are buried, hopes are born,
  And power prophetic utters
The coming glory. Heaven and Earth
  Pulse with impatient fervour,
And reborn Nature hymns her mirth
  To VISHNU THE PRESERVER!

There's my apology for the poor Hindoos:
Convert them, if you can, but do not damn;
Curse not the beggar when you dole your doit;
Preach, like St. Paul, in gentlemanly wise,
And do not swear that brindled hides are black
To make yourself look whiter. I believe
There is much high and holy wisdom hid

Sancte Socrates, ora pro Nobis!

DEAR God, by wrathful routs
  How is thy Church divided;
And how may he that doubts
  In such turmoil be guided!
When weeping I behold
  How Christian people quarrel,
Ofttimes from Heathens old
  I fetch a saintly moral;
And while they fret with rage
  The sore-distraught community,
I look for some Greek sage
  Who preaches peace and unity.
      And thus I pray:

O Sancte Socrates, ora pro nobis!
Let faith and love and joy increase,
And reason rule and wrangling cease,
Good saint, we pray thee!

They pile a priestly fence
Of vain scholastic babble,
To keep out common sense
With the unlearnèd rabble.
A curious creed they weave,
And, for the Church commands it,
All men must needs believe,
Though no man understands it;
Thus, while they rudely ban
All honest thought as treason,
I from the Heathen clan
Seek solace to my reason,
And thus I pray:
O Sancte Socrates, ora pro nobis!
From creeds that men believe because

They fear a damnatory clause,
Good saint, deliver us!

Some preach a God so grim
That, when his anger swelleth,
They crouch and cower to him
When sacred fear compelleth;
God loves his few pet lambs,
And saves his one pet nation,
The rest he largely damns
With swinging reprobation.
Thus banished from the fold,
I wisely choose to follow
Some sunny preacher old
Who worshipped bright Apollo;
And thus I pray:
O Sancte Socrates, ora pro nobis!
From silly flocks of petted lambs,
And from a faith that largely damns,
Good saint, deliver us!

And some do strongly strive
  By light of noonday taper,
The guilty soul to shrive
  With many a gest and caper;
With candlestick and bells,
  With postures and grimaces,
With wealth of holy spells,
  And lack of lovely graces;
And when I see increase
  These feats of antic duty,
I turn me back to Greece
  Where truth was wed to beauty,
      And thus I pray:
O Sancte Socrates, ora pro nobis!
  From quaint religion tricked in laces,
  From genuflexions and grimaces,
    Good saint, deliver us!

And some there be that say,
  That through their veins a virtue

The Hope of the Heterodox.

IN Thee, O blessed God, I hope,
In Thee, in Thee, in Thee!
Though banned by Presbyter and Pope,
My trust is still in Thee.
Thou wilt not cast Thy servant out
Because he chanced to see
With his own eyes, and dared to doubt
What praters preach of Thee.
O no! no! no!
For ever and ever, and aye
(Though Pope and Presbyter bray)
Thou wilt not cast away
An honest soul from Thee.

I look around on earth and sky,
  And Thee, and ever Thee,
With open heart and open eye
  How can I fail to see?
My ear drinks in from field and fell
  Life's rival floods of glee:
Where finds the priest his private hell
  When all is full of Thee?
      O no! no! no!
    Though flocks of sacred geese
    Give Heaven's high ear no peace.
    I still enjoy a lease
      Of happy thoughts from Thee.

My faith is strong; out of itself
  It grows erect and free;
No Talmud on the Rabbi's shelf
  Gives amulets to me.

Small Greek I know, nor Hebrew much,
  But this I plainly see.
Two legs without the Bishop's crutch
  God gave to thee and me.
      O no! no! no!
    The Church may loose and bind,
    But MIND, immortal Mind,
    As free as wave or wind
      Came forth, O God, from Thee.

O pious quack! thy pills are good,
  But mine as good may be,
And healthy men on healthy food
  Live without you or me.
Good lady! let the doer do!
  Thought is a busy bee,
Nor honey less what it doth brew,
  Though very gall to thee.
      O no! no! no!

Though Councils decree and declare,
Like a tree in open air
The soul its foliage fair
  Spreads forth, O God, to Thee!

O Hear my Prayer!

O HEAR my prayer,
If I may dare
To talk with Thee, Great Spirit,
Of mortal mould,
To frailty sold,
Who dust and death inherit!

What thing am I
To soar so high,
Such proud conceits to cherish?—
An insect born
With dewy morn,
With dewy eve to perish.

Yet am I not
By Thee forgot,
Thou knowest not forgetting;
The perfect All
Nor great nor small
Nor rising knows nor setting.

One ocean rolls
Whose waves are souls,
With radiant-shifting features;
That ocean Thou,
Eternal NOW,
The shifting waves Thy creatures.

When Thou art nigh
We live; we die
From Thy sustainment sundered;
Even as the spark
Goes out in dark
That from its flame hath wandered.

Therefore no harm
That wingèd worm
Should lofty fancies cherish;
Or great or small,
On Him hangs all,
Who lives and cannot perish.

And I will dare
To lift my prayer
With trust in Thee, Great Spirit,
By whose high might
Day springs from Night
And Death doth Life inherit.

The Sabbath Day.

THE Sabbath-day, the Sabbath-day,
  How softly shines the morn!
How gently from the heathery brae
  The fresh hill-breeze is borne!
Sweetly the village bell doth toll,
  And thus it seems to say,
Come rest thee, rest thee, weary soul,
  On God's dear Sabbath-day!

Swift as the shifting pictures flit
  Unscanned, unnoticed by,
To those who in the steam-car sit
  And pass with rapid eye;

So flits our life with sweeping haste,
And hath no power to stay;
But GOD makes man His favoured guest
On each dear Sabbath-day:

And to high converse doth invite
The soul with tranquil eye
That numbers well, and marks aright
The moments as they fly;
The soul that will not lawless roam,
Nor with blind hurry stray,
But with itself would be at home
On a peaceful Sabbath-day.

There are who live as in a fair,
The light, the shallow-hearted,
Nor ask or whither bound, or where
They stand, or whence they started;
Aimless they live, and thoughtless fling
Their rattling lives away,

Nor know to poise the brooding wing
  On a sober Sabbath-day.

Such judge I not. But me not so
  GOD made for light-winged prattle:
A soldier I, and I must know
  Before I fight, my battle.
I with the jingling bells an hour
  Would sport, then steal away,
To feel with truth, and plan with power,
  On a thoughtful Sabbath-day.

Stern Scottish people, ye redeem
  Each seventh day severely;
Sober and grave, with scarce a gleam
  Of frolic tempered cheerly.
Light wits deride your thoughtful law,
  The tinkling and the gay;
But wisely from deep founts ye draw
  Calm strength on the Sabbath-day.

And safely, if I err, I err,
  Who on this day with you
The hot-spurred bustle and the stir
  Of dinsome life eschew;
Happy, if through the frequent dark
  Of man's tumultuous way,
God in my soul shall light a spark
  On His dear Sabbath-day.

Rullion Green.

HERE, on this height, where pastoral Pentland
falls,
With easy slope, into the Lothian plain,
Where silence fills the azure-vaulted halls,
And solitude's serenest soul doth reign ;
Where scarce the pewit's shrill far-plaining cry
Disturbs the quiet sleep o' the hill breeze,
And the bare brae seems clad, in mockery,
With one thin belt of lean and scurvy trees ;
Here let me pause : Here mighty deeds were done
By Scotland's sires ; and I am Scotland's son.

Say not that they were harsh, and stern, and sour,
Or say they were so, but not therefore base ;

In iron times God sends, with mighty power,
  Iron apostles to make smooth His ways;
And hearts of rock, close-clamped with many a bar,
  He plants where angry billows lash the shore;
Thus love by fear, thus peace is pledged by war,
  (Stern law!) and gospel paths are paved in gore:
We reap in ease what they did sow in toil,
And rate them harsh, and stern, and sour the while.

I blame them that they were not stern enough,
  Too tamely bore, and waited overlong.
They should have checked, with sharp severe rebuff,
  In the first threshold of his impious wrong,
The pedant-king, whose rash conceit did ween
  With statute-work to stop the strong full heart
God-moved. He fell; and in his fall was seen
  Man less than God, and nature more than art;
Old text, which many wars have preached, and more
Shall write in blood, ere folly's reign be o'er.

Here, on this slope, the Covenanting men
  Stood, lifting holy hearts and holy hands;
And from the hill they looked, with eager ken,
  To catch the nearing of their brother'd bands.
From Teviot's banks, from high Dunedin's brow,
  Some aid was promised, and they hoped for more;
But ah! it was too bold a venture now,
  And hands were weak, where tongues were strong
      before:
Dunedin closed her ports; and from the west
Hung grim Dalziel, avoidless as the pest.

But fear they knew not. With an holy bond
  In Clydesdale they had bound them to their God;
Nor do their hearts in danger's hour despond,
  They bear Heaven's mandate, and they own its
      nod.
Beneath the cold and clear November noon,
  Their hearts beat high upon the lonely hill;

Souls mild and kindly as the leafy June,
Stood cased in stern resolve, and dauntless will;
And, when soft pity melts the mood severe,
There God doth paint a rainbow in each tear.

Hark, from the hill ascends the solemn chant!
And hark again the startling war-cry rings!
A mud-splashed rider comes with breathless pant—
'’Tis he, the grim Dalziel, and death he brings
Or to himself, or you!'—Straightway were heard
The hungry hell-hounds through the stony dell
Hurrying. Their swords the godly warriors gird,
With godly benediction bless them well;
Then rush to the fray. The hostile horse they beat
Back to the glen, with swift severe retreat.

And yet again the clattering onset came;
And yet again they drave it back in blood;
But grim Dalziel, now burning with fierce flame,
Gathered his serried hundreds. Like a flood,

He rolled, and swept the rankless tens away,
  Whose valour now was bootless. They so few
Had boldly hoped to keep a host at bay;
Nor vainly—had their plighted friends been true.
Not lack of heart, but lack of ordered skill,
And lack of needful aidance wrought their ill.

Rude warriors, rest! God from that ill wrought good;
  Your strong endurance wrought strong hate of
    wrong,
Let dark Dunnottar's dungeon-solitude,
  And the strong Bass, attest your sufferings long;
No polished pen, no smooth and courtly verse,
  Ye need to prove the virtue of your crime;
Pentland's green slopes, and the bleak moors o' the
    Merse,
  Shall be your record to remotest time;
Ourselves, your sons, inheriting your stuff,
While we are worthy, shall be praise enough;

As ye were worthy of the royal man
  Whose battle-axe the English epicure
Clove with a stroke, when the first fray began
  At glorious Bannockburn! The purple moor,
While 'tis our home, the high hills granite-bound,
  Shall brace our hearts, and make us valiant men;
From every crag a hero's tale shall sound,
  A holy warning echo from each glen.
Shall slaves be dull where Wallace' blade was keen?
Shall sleeve and surplice flaunt o'er Rullion Green?

Needs not this rhyme to tell their pious roll,
  Who slept in caves, and on bleak hills did preach;
Guthrie, M'Kail, strong hearts that scorned control,
  The soldier Wallace, many-wandering Veitch.
These sure did share His brotherhood sincere,
  The Christ, who had not where to lay His head:
He died for all; for some who haply jeer
  They in this clay did make their gory bed;

Men rude and wild, rough, shaggy, and uncouth,
But true and honest, and who died for truth.

Thou, Scotland's son, that wouldst be leal and true,
  This storied stone, not dry and tearless scan:
Bleed for their wounds who freely bled for you,
  And know how good, how great a thing is man.
O these did boast no brightly barren deed!
  One death for freedom makes a million free;
And who achieves a self-dependent creed,
  Has gained Mind's first and last great victory;
Gains more than hero's, more than bard's renown—
'GOD'S SAINTS DIED HERE, AND GAINED THE MARTYR'S CROWN.'

Lines written at Magus Muir.

LAMENT who will the surplice rent,
And mitre trampled low,
I cannot think the blow mis-spent,
That felled our priestly foe.

Who sent him here?—a perjured king.
His work?—with churchman's art
To bind young Freedom's mounting wing,
And crush a people's heart.

Ill-omened priest! for courtly place
Well made, and cold propriety;
But here thou found'st a fervid race,
Whose sternly-glowing piety

Scorned paper laws. Their free-bred soul
  Went not with priests to school,
To trim the tippet and the stole,
  And pray by printed rule;

But they would cast the eager word,
  From their heart's fiery core,
Smoking and red, as God had stirred
  The Hebrew men of yore.

And thou didst come, a cassocked slave,
  With windy proclamation,
Parchment, and ink, and wax, to brave
  The spirit of a nation;

And with rash plume didst brush the flame,
  And wert consumed, poor fly!—
So perish all, who join the name
  Of Christ, with tyranny!

Prate not of law and lawyer's art!
When kingly sin is rife,
The law is in a people's heart,
That whets the needful knife.

O Scotland! O my country! thou
Through blood hast waded well;
From glorious Bannockburn till now,
The tyrant hears his knell

Rung from thy iron heart. And we,
In lone rock-girdled glen,
Or purple heath, erect and free,
From harsh knife-bearing men

Inherit peace. Lament who will
The mitre trampled low;
Not all are murderers who kill,
The cause commends the blow.

Martin Luther.

WHO sits upon the Pontiff's throne?
On Peter's holy chair
Who sways the keys? At such a time
When dullest ears may hear the chime
Of coming thunders—when dark skies
Are writ with crimson prophecies,
A wise man should be there;
A godly man, whose life might be
The living logic of the see;
One quick to know, and keen to feel,
A fervid man, and full of zeal,
Should sit in Peter's chair.

Alas! no fervid man is there,
  No earnest, honest heart;
But one who, dress'd in priestly guise,
Looks on the world with worldling's eyes;
One who can trim the courtier's smile,
Or weave the diplomatic wile,
  But knows no deeper art;
One who can dally with fair forms,
Whom a well-pointed period warms—
No man is he to hold the helm
Where rude winds blow, and wild waves whelm,
  And creaking timbers start.

In vain did Julius pile sublime
  The vast and various dome,
That makes the kingly pyramids' pride,
And the huge Flavian wonder hide
Their heads in shame—these gilded stones
(O heaven!) were very blood and bones
  Of souls whom Christ did come

To save—vile gain of knaves who sold
Celestial rights for earthy gold,
Marketing grace with merchant's measure,
To prank with Europe's pillaged treasure
  The pride of purple Rome!

The measure of her sins is full,
  The scarlet-vested whore!
Thy murderous and lecherous race
Have sat too long i' the holy place;
The knife shall lop what no drug cures;
Nor Heaven permits, nor earth endures,
  The monstrous mockery more.
Behold! I swear it, saith the Lord:
Mine elect warrior girds the sword;
A nameless man, a miner's son,
Shall tame thy pride, thou haughty one,
  And pale the painted whore!

Earth's mighty men are naught. I chose
  Poor fishermen before,

To preach my gospel to the poor;
A pauper boy from door to door
That trolled his hymn—by his strong word
The priest-bound world shall now be stirred,
  As with a lion's roar!
A lonely monk that loved to dwell
With peaceful book in silent cell;
This man shall shake the Pontiff's throne:
Him kings and emperors shall own,
  And stout hearts wince before

The eye profound and lordly front
  Where speculation reigns.
He to the learnèd seats shall climb,
On Science' watch-tower stand sublime;
The arid doctrine shall inspire
Of wiry teachers with swift fire;
  And, piled with cumbrous pains
Proud palaces of sounding lies
Lay prostrate with a breath. The wise

Shall listen to his word; the youth
Shall eager seize the new-born truth,
  Where prudent age refrains.

Lo! where the venal pomp proceeds
  From echoing town to town!
The clamorous preacher and his train,
Organ and bell with sound inane,
The crimson cross, the book, the keys,
The flag that spreads before the breeze,
  The triple-belted crown!
It wends its way; and straw is sold,
Yea! deadly drugs for heavy gold,
To feeble hearts whose pulse is fear;
And though some smile, and many sneer,
  There's none will dare to frown.

None dares but one—the race is rare—
  One free and honest man:
Truth is a dangerous thing to say

When high-throned falsehoods rule the day;
But He hath lent it voice; and, lo!
From heart to heart the fire shall go,
  And fuse with plastic plan.
Proud bishops with a lordly train,
Fierce cardinals with high disdain,
Sleek chamberlains with smooth discourse,
And wrangling doctors, all shall force
  In vain, one honest man.

In vain the foolish Pope shall fret;
  It is a sober thing,
Thou high-blown trifler! cease to rave,
Loudly to damn, and loudly save,
Sweeping with mimic thunders' swell
Armies of honest souls to hell!
  The time on rushing wing
Hath fled when this prevailed. O, Heaven!
One hour, one little hour, is given,
If thou couldst but repent. But no!

To ruin thou shalt headlong go,
  A doomed and blasted thing.

Thy parchment ban comes forth; and lo!
  Men heed it not, thou fool!
See, from the learnèd city's gate,
In solemn show, in pomp of state,
The watchmen of the truth come forth,
The burghers old of sterling worth,
  And students of the school:
And he who should have felt thy ban,
Walks like a prophet in the van;
He hath a calm untroubled look,
Beneath his arm he bears a book,
  And in his hand the Bull.

He halts; and in the middle space
  Bids pile a blazing fire.
The flame ascends with crackling glee;
Then, with firm step advancing, he

Gives to the wild fire's wasting rule
The false Decretals, and the Bull,
  While thus he vents his ire :—
'Because the Holy One o' the Lord
Thou vexèd hast with impious word,
Therefore the Lord shall thee consume,
And thou shalt share the Devil's doom
  In everlasting fire !'

He said; and rose the echo round
  'In everlasting fire !'
The hearts of men were free; one word
Their inner depths of soul had stirred;
Erect before their God they stood
A truth-shod Christian brotherhood,
  And winged with high desire.
And ever with the circling flame
Uprose anew the blithe acclaim :—
'The righteous Lord shall thee consume,
And thou shalt share the Devil's doom
  In everlasting fire !'

Thus the brave German men. And we
  Shall echo back the cry.
The burning of that parchment scroll
Annulled the bond that thralled the soul
Of man to man; each brother now
Only to one great Lord will bow,
  One Father-God on high.
And though with fits of lingering life
The wounded foe prolong the strife,
On Luther's deed we build our hope,
Having this seal—the fond old Pope
  Is dying, and shall die.

Patrick Hamilton.

IN St. Andrew's grey-towered city
Once was done a deed unholy,
When the harsh and haughty churchman
Crushed the martyr meek and lowly.
Young was he, and gentle-thoughted,
Blood of kings flowed in his veins;
But with manly mild endurance
Stout he bore the fiery pains.
And he gave his life a priceless
Ransom, to make Scotland free,
By the faith which scorns the fagot,
Bloody priest of Rome, from thee.
Hoar St. Andrews, thou didst witness,
When the dark-stoled priestly crew

Came swift trooping, where the trumpet
  Of the far-feared Beaton blew.
Thou didst see the mitred council
  Sit, and, with a ghastly prayer,
Pray the God who loves his creatures
  To make foulest murder fair
With holy names; and thou didst hear it
  When, instead of reasons true,
Age gave grace to doting dogma,
  Truth was damned because 'twas new.
And for burning words heart-kindling,
  Soulless creeds were grimly read
From books, that with a monstrous learning
  Slaved the living to the dead.
They with sounding pomp disputed,
  Meekly he, and calmly wise;
They with curious deft manœuvre,
  He with short plain text replies.
Forth then went that calm refuter,
  While they muttered spiteful wrath,

And the mob, with senseless clamour,
  Hooted round his guiltless path.
To the place of doom they led him,
  In his hand the holiest book;
Bright the noon-day sun was shining,
  Brighter shone the martyr's look.
To the bloody stake they bound him
  With strong bonds, who needed none;
Freely to the fiery torture
  Marched the noble Hamilton.
Blessings for their hateful curses
  He returned; his voice implored
Pardon to his stone-eyed murderers,
  While the blazing billet roared.
God was with him in his anguish,
  Jesus gave him strength divine;
He, like Stephen, saw the glory
  Through the wreathèd darkness shine.
And a glorious light behind him
  Shone—and shines—whose death made free

Scotland, spite of fire and fagot,
  Bloody priest of Rome, from thee!
And the towers of grey St. Andrews,
  By the roaring German wave,
While we name his name shall teach us
  To be gentle, true, and brave.

Walter Myln.

Non nostra impietas, aut actæ crimina vitæ
Armarunt hostes in mea fata truces,
Sola fides Christi, sacris signata libellis,
Quæ vitæ causa est, est mihi causa necis.

Epitaph on Myln by PATRICK ADAMSON,
Archbishop of St. Andrews.

ONE breezy day, when all the sea was white
With hoary crests, that rose upon the brine,
Like ruffled plumes upon a fretted bird,
Behind St. Andrews old grey towers I stood,
And paced with pensive foot the high-raised walk,
Which northward looks across the bay, to where
The far red headland, eastward stretching, flouts
The keen dry blast. As I was musing there

Of ancient times and new, bishops and priests,
Martyrs and saints, and sage philosophers,
And bright-eyed dames, who shine in learning's halls,
Like gay birds flitting through a dusky grove;
There comes before my path a little man,
Smooth and close-shaven, very trig and smug,
And well-appointed, not a speck of dust
On all his long black coat, which down beneath
His slender hams, near to his ankle fell;
A snow-white neckcloth with a dainty tie
Embraced his neck, whose skin was fair and fine
As any damsel's :—with a simpering lisp
He spake, and asked me—Pray, Sir, can you tell
What man was Walter Myln? I, like a Scot,
Replied—Why ask you that? I read, quoth he,
That name upon the obelisk, which stands
High-perched above the benty golfing ground,
And, being here a stranger, fain would know
What names you honour in this Northern land;
Our saints in Oxford have a larger fame,

And sound through time, their own interpreter.
O yes! I said, you Southern Square-caps know
As much of Scotland, as a fly that 's bred
In a grocer's sugar-cask may comprehend
Of honeyed heather and of mountain bees.
Our glens, you deem, are pleasant hunting-ground
For London brewers and ducal debauchees,
And our fair lochs and mountains a rare show
To salve blear eyes, sick with a six months' view
Of peevish faces in a hot saloon!
But, since your question hints some stray regard
For Scottish worthies, and the sacred blood
That glued the stones of our stout Scottish Kirk,
I 'll tell you what I know,—though, in good sooth,
Not much is known of Myln, and even that little
By flippant wits is mostly overskipped,
Whose eye is all for courts and cavaliers,
Crowns, mitres, coronets, and gaudy crests,
Stars, crosses, ribbons, painted heraldries,
The pomp and flare of life; but quiet worth

In strong-souled martyr, or meek-suffering saint,
Like some fair flower in hollow glen remote,
Finds not their roving eye. So said, I drew
A circle round my thoughts, and them adjured
To do their master's will; and to the smug,
Smooth-lipped Oxonian thus my tale began:
Myln, like most men, in those unbookish days,
Who had no taste for arms, was bred to the Church;
And as our Scotland lies remote, a small
Creek in the wide sea of the world, where tides
Are latest felt, he sailed abroad, and spread
The germing blossoms of his youthful thought,
To burst before the doctors of Almayne,
Most learned and subtle. There, belike, his ear
Caught the first stirrings of the God-sent gale,
Which, blown tempestuous from the shrilling trump
Of a poor Saxon monk, smote branchy Rome
With dwindling fear, and from the roots uptore
Her pride o'er half the world. Thence he returned,
Stirred by new thoughts, and thrilled by poignant doubts,

To his dear Scotland, where for many years
The daily offices of the church he used,
And plied the faithful round of priestly service,
In Lunan's sandy bay. The outward man
Long time was calm ; but still the ferment worked
Of the new doctrine, which the times had imped
Into his budding soul, and his heart swayed
With strange discomfort; till his ripened thoughts
Grew larger than his place, and he must burst
Old bonds of life. Then, like an embryo bird,
One day—he knew not how, but God that morn
Had pricked his soul—he cracked his shelly case,
Claimed his due portion in a larger life,
And stood a freeman in a land of slaves.
Like as a man, who, in some dusty nook
Of an old lumber-room, amid a heap
Of yellowed papers, lavishly bescrawled
With silly records of ephemeral loves,
And trivial sorrows, suddenly hath spied
A parchment signed and sealed, whose stamp revives

Lost claims, his rusted right refurbishes,
And makes him lord of long mislorded roods ;
Into new life he starts, surveys the world
With bolder scope, breathes a more ample breath,
And stands a peer, who late had crouched a slave :
Even so this simple priest, before the power
Of misvouched creeds and a mistutored church,
Stood, with the new-found Bible in his hand,
Which God's own finger wrote.—Forthwith he went,
And preached the precious truth he knew to all,
As free as he had found it ; but not all
Would gladly hear it. Few had wit to know ;
And of these few, the fewest with strong nerve
Could bear the radiant truth, but dubious lived,
Fearing the dark, and blinking at the day.
Who flings broad truth into a falsèd age
Must count his foes by thousands, and his friends
By units. So, indeed, the priesthood raised
About poor Myln a clattering hue and cry,
As he were known a thief, and rent the ears

O' the fevered time with fretful bickerment;
And him at length in Dysart town—a place
More bruited then than now—they rudely seized,
And to St. Andrews hoary castle haled,
And barred him in yon tower beside the sea,
Whose dungeon yet smelt rank with innocent blood
Of Wishart, and the noble Hamilton.
There first with baits of fleshly lure they tipped
Their churchly hooks, and promised him a stall
In rich Dunfermline's abbey, there to live
In fatted comfort, and to slide at ease
Into a cushioned grave. But not such man
Such straw might tickle. So, from prison dragged,
Before the assembly of the priests he stood,
Even in the pulpit of the Bishop's church
Impeached of heresy; and fearless there
With meek aspect fronted the proud array
Of priests and bishops, priors, provosts, all
The knighthood of the Pope, with motley troops
Of friars, black, and white, and grey, as thick

As flies, that on a sweltering summer day
Have scented carrion in a clover field—
Even in the great church metropolitan
He in the pulpit stood, a weak old man,
But firm, with face serene, and shaded soft
With the mild dignity of fourscore years,
To answer for his faith. They on a bench
Sate lofty-throned, and with full lofty looks
Surveyed the people, or with face composed
To meek devotion, while high-vaulting pride
Housed in their hearts; some only fat and dull,
And gross with swinish habitude of soul,
That made them grunt, when any cleanly foot
Intruded on their sty. Before such court
Sworn in God's name, and to their murtherous work
Invoking Father, Son, and Holy Ghost,
Stood Walter Myln. How they accused him, what
The counts of his offending, you may read
In Foxe's book of gospel witnesses;
How he had dared, as any creature dares,

To find a mate, and mingle with his like;
How he had said that bread was bread, not flesh,
And wine plain wine, not very blood of God;
How he declared that bishops were no bishops,
Who marketed in holy things, to feed
Not Christ's dear flock, but their own pride; and how
From land to land he pilgrimed, not to kiss
The bones of maundering monks, and patter prayers
To swart-faced Maries prinked with trumperies,
But with free power to preach the eternal law
Of truth and love, and righteousness to men!
All this he patient heard, and inly wept
To think that reasoning men should reason use,
To lift flat nonsense into attitudes
Of lofty sense, strutting on learnèd stilts,
And weaving curious webs of twisted phrase,
Not to reveal the truth, but to conceal.
Then, when their talk was done, he rose, and flung
Their trivial charges from his swelling soul,
Like straw before the wind; for God inspired

The old man's heart with breath of truth, that he,
His hot youth boiling in his aged breast,
Made nave and choir to ring and sound again,
So stoutly he protested. Wilt thou recant?
Quoth Oliphant—so hight the questioning clerk—
If not, the fire is waiting; thou shalt die.
Then calmly thus the old man spake: I STAND
ACCUSED OF LIFE. I KNOW THAT I MUST DIE,
SOME DAY NOT DISTANT. THEREFORE WHAT YOU DO,
DO QUICKLY. PROVE ME. I WILL NOT RECANT
GOD'S TRUTH; FOR I AM CORN; I AM NO CHAFF.
NEITHER WITH WIND SHALL I BE BLOWN AWAY,
NOR BURST BY FLAIL; BUT I WILL BOTH ABIDE.
And so he made his brave confession, words
Worth libraries of tinkling rhetoric,
Words that made Scotland free, and eftsoons drave
The tyrannous Pope and all his company
Of mitred hirelings from our ransomed land.
But first he gave, like Socrates, his life
To pledge his words; and so with gore they shent

His silvery locks, and for a winding-sheet
Swathed him in flaming pitch; yet not without
Deep grudge of honest men. The people's heart
Was sick of blood, nor wished the old man dead.
The minions of the priesthood were constrained—
For none would lend a rope—to cut the cords
Of their own tents, to bind him to the stake;
Where being fixed, he stood like one entranced
With holy rapture and serene discourse.
Yet not with dumb submission died; once more,
While life remained, and the keen-crackling blaze
Choked not his utterance, his free voice he raised
For truth and right, and God and Christ. And all
The people's hearts were moved; and many wept—
Though tears were perilous then—and inly curst
The priestly bonds they had no strength to break.

And so my tale was told. I saw my smooth
Oxonian friend had only half a mind
To hear my story out; for these Square-caps

Give their free right hand to the Pope, to us
With grudging grace their left; but I was pleased
To blurt a dash of broad-cast Scottish truth,
Athwart his lisping lips. Well, well! he says,
You Scotsmen are a pertinacious brood,
And have that harsh-grained stuff in you, which makes
Bigots and martyrs, democrats and bores;
Fitly you wear the thistle in your cap,
As in your grim theology! I laughed.
O we're not all so fierce! God knows, you'll find
Well-combed and smooth-licked gentlemen enough
In our saloons, who will rejoice with you
To sneer at massive Calvin's close-wedged creed,
And deem John Knox a boor, who dared to speak
Truth to a pretty face topped with a crown;
Who hold that preachers should, like peers, avouch
Their right to preach, by links of pedigree
From Paul or Peter; whom a fervid prayer,
Or a bold word turns to nice squeamishness;
Who sigh for liturgies and surplices,

And all the frippery of your silken church !
Fear not !—the memory of our iron times
Frets the fine nerves of this soft-nurtured age.
Our very streets are prankt with Prelacy ;
The squares of breezy Edinburgh show
Statues to perjured princes, men who lived
Chief captains of a swinish court, and died
With rotten souls embalmed in Popery.
Proud monuments are piled to eternise
Lawyers with supple conscience and glib tongue
And frizzled kings, with never a deeper thought
Than their rolled waistcoats—but you'll beat in vain
Those streets to find one stone to memorise
Dauntless John Knox, or faithful Walter Myln.

So my Scotch bile I vented ; and our ways
We parted : he across the golfing ground,
Whence blew the railway's screeching whistle ; I
To hold discourse with sage philosophers
Of knowing and of being, and to feed

Mine eyes with pleasant play of kindly looks
From bright-eyed dames, who shine in learning's
halls,
Like gay birds flitting through a dusky grove.

The Generous Evangelist.[1]

WELL, friend, I see thy soul is hushed;
Methought thine eye was weeping,
Then when the strong-winged preacher rushed,
With thunders in his keeping,

Athwart thy thought. Thou doest
'Tis rare that English eyes
Thaw at the pulpit's potent spell;
They are too coldly wise.

But thou this day hast seen and felt,
In worship's solemn hour,
How in the rough-hewn Scotsman dwelt
The Word of God with power.

[1] The original of this picture is the late THOMAS GUTHRIE, the eloquent apostle of the Ragged Schools.

No lawn-sleeved gospeller he ; no trim
  Vender of church proprieties,
Whence delicate lips may learn to brim
  With nice new mixed varieties

Of sacerdotal phrase. Not he,
  For every human need,
With clipping tongue doth guarantee
  The stamped and labelled creed

Of statutable faith ; but strong
  In the rude strength of Nature,
Amid the motley human throng,
  He plants his manly stature,

And flings the wingèd Word abroad,
  With large and liberal grace,
As one that hath conversed with God :
  Such glory fills his face.

O 'tis a noble sight to see
  A strong fresh-hearted man,
From the cramped orthodoxy free
  Of the square school-bred clan,

Preach Christ's pure gospel! Why should men
  With bristling terminology
Of things beyond all human ken
  Fence round divine theology?

This man smells not of books. A green
  And lusty show he bears;
As one whose foot hath wandering been
  Where vitalising airs

Sweep the far-purpled hills. His God
  He cabins not in creeds;
But feels him where the fir-trees nod,
  And where the South wind speeds

O'er blossomy fields. In waves and winds
  For gospel texts he looks;
And in the hearts of men he finds
  What no man found in books.

His doctrines from the streets he brings;
  From ploughman's lowly cot,
From proud palatial halls of kings,
  From dens where sinners rot

In darkness and disease. He hath
  The wise man's art to borrow
From others' life; he treads the path
  Of each man's joy and sorrow,

Even as a brother. What all feel
  He speaks; and all men see
The thoughts their own dim hearts reveal
  Glow with new radiancy

In his strong glass. As lovers see
  Their wish displayed in lovers,
So to each God-moved spirit he
  The God-ward path discovers.

Would there were many such! But we
  By narrow walls are bounded
Of sundered life: so large and free,
  So full, yet unconfounded,

Are few. The most shape forth a shell
  Of narrow notions crude,
And in this self-spun prison dwell,
  Strange to all foreign good.

Dear friend, our Scotch creed is severe,
  I grant; but Christianity
Hath found one strong mild champion here
  Who stirs our deep humanity,

And makes the blessèd tears to flow,
  The fount of holy sorrow,
Which if thou cherish well, thou 'lt know
  A clearer life to-morrow.

Thank Heaven, thou 'rt richer grown this day,
  By one great fact at least;
And all who wept with thee may say—
  'HERE SPAKE A GENEROUS PRIEST!'

Benedicite.

German Air—*Alles Schweige!*

ANGELS holy,
High and lowly,
Sing the praises of the Lord!
Earth and sky, all living nature,
Man, the stamp of thy Creator,
Praise ye, praise ye, God the Lord!

Sun and moon bright,
Night and noonlight,
Starry temples azure-flooded,
Cloud and rain, and wild winds' madness,
Breeze that floats with genial gladness,
Praise ye, praise ye, God the Lord!

Ocean hoary,
Tell His glory,
Cliffs, where tumbling seas have roared!
Pulse of waters blithely beating,
Wave advancing, wave retreating,
Praise ye, praise ye, God the Lord!

Rock and high land,
Wood and island,
Crag where eagle's pride hath soared,
Mighty mountains purple-breasted,
Peaks cloud-heaving, snowy-crested,
Praise ye, praise ye, God the Lord!

Rolling river,
Praise Him ever,
From the mountain's deep-vein poured;
Silver fountain clearly gushing,
Troubled torrent madly rushing,
Praise ye, praise ye, God the Lord!

Bond and free man,
Land and sea man,
Earth with peoples widely stored,
Wanderer lone o'er prairies ample,
Full-voiced choir in costly temple,
Praise ye, praise ye, God the Lord!

Praise Him ever,
Bounteous Giver!
Praise Him, Father, Friend, and Lord!
Each glad soul its free course winging,
Each blithe voice its free song singing,
Praise the great and mighty Lord!

Songs of Life.

The River: an Allegory of Life.

I.

SON of the mountain am I,
  Born 'twixt the Earth and the Sky,
Where kindly cherished I lay
In my cradle of soft mossy green,
Looking with clear bright eye
On the clouds that curtained the day,
Floating in freakish display
With cerulean glimpses between.
  Son of the mountain am I,
  Born 'twixt the Earth and the Sky,
Where the old grey rocks stand out

'Mid the tempest's revel and rout,
Snorting with jagged old snout
  At the keen winds whistling by;
Where the eagle spreads his van,
And the white-winged ptarmigan—
  Fed by rich dews from the sky
  There an infant of might I did lie.

II.

Young was I, and lusty-hearted,
When first from the mountain I started,
  Down from the Ben's grey shoulders
  Over the old granite boulders,
  Scornful of rest and of ease,
Eagerly running and leaping,
Scooping the rocks with my sweeping,
  Tearing the roots of the trees;
Swelling with torrent big-breasted,
Dashing with stream foamy-crested

Mighty and masterful then:
      Heaving and hurling,
      Whirling and swirling
O'er the harsh roots of the Ben;
      Foaming and bubbling,
      Winding and doubling
Through the long stretch of the glen,
      So lusty was I,
      Son of Earth and of Sky,
So proud of my potency then!

III.

Now I am grown to a River,
   With measured and equable strain
Rolling my waters, and never
   To toss and to tumble again;
I am grown to a smooth-flooded River,
The mighty and merciful Giver
   Of wealth to the sons of the plain.

Through meadows and terraces pleasant
  In triumph of culture I ride,
With the home of the peer and the peasant
  To bless the rich roll of my tide;
The firm-poised bridge I flow under,
  The fair-builded city I know,
And spires, domes, and turrets, a wonder,
  Nod their pride in my glass as I go;
And high-tunnelled vessels are steaming
  And churning the foam of my tide,
And trafficking thousands are streaming
  With quick-eyed despatch at my side.
And millions are praising the River
  As he regally rolls to the main,
The mighty and merciful Giver
  Of wealth to the sons of the plain.

Beautiful World.

BEAUTIFUL world!
    Though bigots condemn thee,
My tongue finds no words
    For the graces that gem thee!
Beaming with sunny light,
    Bountiful ever,
Streaming with gay delight,
    Full as a river!
        Bright world! brave world!
            Let cavillers blame thee!
        I bless thee, and bend
            To the God who did frame thee!

Beautiful world!
  Bursting around me,
Manifold, million-hued
  Wonders confound me!
From earth, sea, and starry sky,
  Meadow and mountain,
Eagerly gushes
  Life's magical fountain.
        Bright world! brave world!
          Though witlings may blame thee,
        Wonderful excellence
          Only could frame thee!

The bird in the greenwood
  His sweet hymn is trolling,
The fish in blue ocean
  Is spouting and rolling!
Light things on airy wing
  Wild dances weaving,

Clods with new life in spring
  Swelling and heaving !
    Thou quick-teeming world,
      Though scoffers may blame thee,
    I wonder, and worship
      The God who could frame thee !

Beautiful world !
  What poesy measures
Thy strong-flooding passions,
  Thy light-trooping pleasures ?
Mustering, marshalling,
  Striving and straining,
Conquering, triumphing,
  Ruling and reigning !
    Thou bright-armied world !
      So strong, who can tame thee ?
    Wonderful power of God
      Only could frame thee !

Beautiful world!
While godlike I deem thee,
No cold wit shall move me
With bile to blaspheme thee!
I have lived in thy light,
And, when Fate ends my story,
May I leave on death's cloud
The bright trail of life's glory!
Wondrous old world!
No ages shall shame thee!
Ever bright with new light
From the God who did frame thee!

Moments.

IN the beauty of life's budding,
  When young pulses beat with hope,
And a purple light is flooding
  Round thought's blossoms as they ope;
When the poet's song is dearest,
  And, where sacred anthems swell,
Every word of power thou hearest
  Holds thy spirit like a spell;
    O these are moments, fateful moments,
    Big with issue—use them well!

When a sudden gust hath tumbled
  Hope's bright architecture down;
When some prouder fair hath humbled
  Thy proud passion with a frown;

When thy dearest friends deceive thee,
  And cold looks thy love repel,
And the bitter humours grieve thee,
  That make God's fair earth a hell;
    O these are moments, trying moments,
    Meant to try thee—use them well!

When a flash of truth hath found thee,
  Where thy foot in darkness trod,
When thick clouds dispart around thee,
  And thou standest nigh to God.
When a noble soul comes near thee,
  In whom kindred virtues dwell,
That from faithless doubts can clear thee,
  And with strengthening love compel;
    O these are moments, rare fair moments;
    Sing and shout, and use them well!

When a haughty threat hath cowed thee,
  And with weak, unmanly shame,

Ignoble thou hast bowed thee
  To the terror of a name;
And then God holds the mirror
  Where thy better self doth dwell,
And thou dost start with terror,
  And thy tears gush like a well;
    O these are moments, blessèd moments;
    Weep and pray, and use them well!

In the pride of thy succeeding,
  When, beneath thy high command,
Every soul must own the leading
  Of thy strong-controlling hand;
When wide cheers of acclamation
  Round thy march of triumph swell,
And the plaudits of a nation
  Every thought of fear expel;
    O these are moments, slippery moments;
    Watch and pray, and use them well!

When the term of life hath found thee,
  And thou smilest upon Fate,
And the golden sheaves around thee
  For the angels' sickle wait;
When the pure love thou achievest
  Doth the mortal pang expel,
And a shining track thou leavest
  To dear friends that love thee well;
    O these are moments, happy moments;
    Bless God, with whom all issues dwell!

Sow not in Sorrow.

AIR—*Freut euch des Lebens.*

SOW not in sorrow,
  Fling your seed abroad, and know
God sends to-morrow
  The rain to make it grow!
    A fool is he his woe who feeds,
    And seeks the thorn by which he bleeds,
    While harmless culled from bloomy meads
      The rose comes to the wise!

    The past no prayer can bring again,
    The future cheats the scheming brain,
    The present with its golden gain
      Is garnered by the wise.

Let each to-morrow
  Do to-morrow's work with power;
But he soweth sorrow
  Who lives beyond the hour.

While mad Ambition stints his sleep,
To scale the skies and plumb the deep,
I trim my little plot, and reap
  My roses with the wise.
Dreams you may borrow,
  From the vasty space around;
My work is thorough,
  In my narrow bound.

The Phrygian Midas prayed of old,
That all he touched might turn to gold.
But thus his dinner, we are told,
  Was lost to him unwise!

He found a sorrow
  Where he hoped a golden joy;
From Midas borrow,
  And be a wiser boy!

When storms with wintry muster come,
And Jove beats loud his thunder drum,
I sit beside the fire and hum
    The song that cheers the wise.
Fear bringeth sorrow;
  'Mid the world's confounding din,
Peace you may borrow
  From faith that's strong within!

When friends are false and patrons frown,
And railway shares go swiftly down,
Weep not! the cross becomes a crown,
    By magic of the wise!

Nurse not your sorrow;
  Though the cloud be dark to-day,
God sends to-morrow
  The bright and cheering ray!

When hireling scribes retail their lies,
And keen the shaft of slander flies,
I see a cherub in the skies
  That smiles upon the wise.
Spur not your sorrow;
  Though the tempest rave to-day,
God sends to-morrow
  The peaceful beaming May.

When juggling statesmen trim their sails
To catch a whiff from shifting gales,
I wait the hour when truth prevails,
  And triumph with the wise.

Dream not to borrow
  Peace from faction's battling waves ;
He reapeth sorrow.
  Who trusts in fools and knaves !

When things once strong go to the wall,
And creeds decay, and churches fall,
What then ? God reigns above them all,
    The Saviour of the wise !
Why should we sorrow,
  When a sphere reels into night ?
God can to-morrow
  Make new worlds more bright.

Thus when the world a-warring goes,
No fretful thorn my finger shows,
While on my breast I wear the rose,
    The star that decks the wise ;

Sow not in sorrow ;
  Fling your seed abroad, and know
God sends to-morrow,
  The rain to make it grow !

The Musical Frogs.[1]

BREKEKEKEX! coax! coax! O happy happy
frogs!
How sweet ye sing! Would God that I
Upon the bubbling pool might lie,
And sun myself to-day
With you! No curtained bride, I ween,
Nor pillowed babe, nor cushioned queen,
Nor tiny fay on emerald green,
Nor silken lady gay,

1 Some dozen or more years ago, while living at Liebenstein, a German hydropathic establishment in Sachse-Meiningen, I took a stroll across the country on a hot summer's day; when coming near some low marshy ground I became aware of a concert of soft musical notes, floating up gently from the pools of water among the reeds. Never having heard anything of the kind before, I went close up to the brink of the water, and soon found that this most sweet discourse came from a colony of green frogs. Their music made such an impression on me, that on the way back to my water-quarters I wrote some lines as a memorandum of the event, and as a sample of the philosophy of enjoyment, in which frogs belike are sometimes wiser than men.

Lies on a softer couch. O Heaven!
How many a lofty mortal, riven
By keen-fanged inflammation,
Might change his lot with yours, to float
On sunny pond with bright green coat,
And sing with gently throbbing throat
Amid the croaking nation,
Brekekekex! coax! coax! O happy happy frogs!

Brekekekex! coax! coax! O happy happy frogs!
Happy the bard who weaves his rhyme
Recumbent on the purple thyme,
In the fragrant month of June;
Happy the sage, whose lofty mood
Doth with far-searching ken intrude
Into the vast infinitude
Of things beyond the moon;
But happier not the wisest man
Whose daring thought leads on the van
Of star-eyed speculation,

Than thou, quick-legged, light-bellied thing,
Within the green pond's reedy ring,
That with a murmurous joy dost sing
        Among the croaking nation,
Brekekekex! coax! coax! O happy happy frogs!

Brekekekex! coax! coax! O happy happy frogs!
Great Jove with dark clouds sweeps the sky,
Where thunders roll and lightnings fly,
        And gusty winds are roaring;
Fierce Mars his stormy steed bestrides,
And, lashing wild its bleeding sides,
O'er dead and dying madly rides,
        Where the iron hail is pouring.
'Tis well; such crash of mighty Powers
Must be: the spell may not be ours
        To tame the hot creation.
But little frogs with paddling foot
Can sing when gods and kings dispute,
And little bards can strum the lute

Amid the croaking nation,
With Brekekekex! coax! coax! O happy happy frogs!

Brekekekex! coax! coax! O happy happy frogs!
Farewell! not always I may sing
Around the green pond's reedy ring
With you, ye boggy Muses!
But I must go and do stern battle
With herds of stiff-necked human cattle,
Whose eager lust of windy prattle
The gentle rein refuses.
O if!—but all such *ifs* are vain;
I'll go and blow my trump again,
With brazen iteration:
And when, by Logic's iron rule,
I've quashed each briskly babbling fool,
I'll seek again your gentle school,
And hum beside the tuneful pool
Amid the croaking nation,
Brekekekex! coax! coax! O happy happy frogs!

The Young Man's Prayer.

From the German of BARON BUNSEN : *written when he was a Student at Göttingen, in the year* 1812, 19*th October.*

THOU, who of what Thou art,
And what Thou dost in boundless space and time,
Didst plant the thought sublime
Deep in the holiest holy of my heart,
That I might well employ
My strength upon Thy praise,
Catching some far ken of Thy glorious ways
Through the long march of the uncounted days,
Drunk with the fulness of exceeding joy;

O draw Thou me
Up to Thy world of bright unhindered sway,

Me the Earth-born, and shake my vision free
From mortal films that blind the face of day!
O hallow Thou my heart,
That I may see some part
Of Thy great glory, as a mortal may!

That me such blessed glimpse may consecrate,
Through all the stumblings of this mortal state,
And float me high
Above the bustle of the driving hour,
Above the passion swelling with mad power,
That, with unwinking eye,
I may behold the surging centuries roll,
Serene with stable soul,
Rooted in Thee, from whom my being came,
Thee, through all time unmoved, and through all change the same!

And, when my thought is laden with rich store,
And my heart streaming o'er

With what Thou art, and what Thou dost, O then
Give Thou my tongue the liberal large employ,
That what I saw. I may make known to men,
  Drunk with the fulness of exceeding joy !

A Song of Three Words.

ORARE, LABORARE, CANTARE.

THREE blissful words I name to thee,
  Three words of potent charm,
From eating care thy heart to free,
  Thy life to shield from harm.
Whoso these blissful words may know
A bold blithe-fronted face shall show,
And shod with peace shall safely go
  Through war and wild alarm.

First ere thy forward foot thou move
  And wield thine arm of might,
Lift up thy heart to Him above
  That all thy ways be right.

To the prime Source of life and power
Let thy soul rise, even as a flower
That skyward climbs in sunny hour
  And seeks the genial light.

Then gird thy loins to manly toil,
  And in the toil have joy :
Greet hardship with a forward smile,
  And love the stern employ.
Thy glory this the harsh to tame,
And by wise stroke and technic flame
In godlike labour's fruitful name
  Old Chaos to destroy.

Then 'mid thy workshop's dusty din,
  Where Titan steam hath sway,
Croon to thyself a song within,
  Or pour the lusty lay ;

Even as a bird that cheerly sings
In narrow cage, nor frets his wings,
But with full-breasted joyance flings
  His soul into the day.

For lofty things let others strive
  With roll of vauntful drum;
Keep thou thy heart, a honeyed hive,
  Like bee with busy hum.
Chase not the bliss with wishful eyes
That ever lures and ever flies,
But in the present joy be wise,
  And let the future come !

Gaudeamus Igitur!

GERMAN AIR.

GAUDEAMUS igitur!
Gaudeamus while you may!
While the fleet hour lightly passes,
Honest men and bonnie lasses,
Breathe unchartered breath to-day!

Gaudeamus igitur!
He is wise who knows to prize
Honest men and bonnie lasses,
Kindly cheer and brimming glasses,
Blooming cheeks and beaming eyes.

Gaudeamus! wouldst thou lightly
Find the charm that saves the wise,
Soar not high to realms supernal,
Dive not down to dens infernal,
Look around with loving eyes!

Gaudeamus! stray not far!
Pleasure walks in trodden ways;
At thy feet the fair flower gather,
Brightest where it grows the heather
Purples all the Highland braes!

Gaudeamus! do not puzzle,
Whence or whither? who can know?
Here we are with hearing, seeing,
To make harvest of our being,
While the summers come and go!

Gaudeamus! who will show us,
Quoth the Psalmist, any good?
Live, and make no curious comment,
Firmly grasp the fruitful moment;
What thy grasp may hold is good.

Gaudeamus! use the present,
In the present there is power;
Honest men and bonnie lasses,
Blooming cheeks and brimming glasses,
That's my gospel for the hour!

A Song of St. Socrates.

Old English Air—*To Anacreon in Heaven.*

I.

To Socrates, seated in bliss with St. Paul,
A club of good fellows sent up a petition,
That they by his name might their brotherhood call,
When this answer came down from the jolly old
Grecian—
Men north of the Tweed,
I wish you God-speed,
You may borrow my name, if you hold by my creed;
And this creed hath been mine,
In bright union to join
Religion and beauty, wit, wisdom, and wine!

II.

I have heard in the skies that you brave Scottish men
For freedom of faith nobly spread out your banners;
This thing I approve; but I shake my head when
They say you are sour and severe in your manners!
Though the thorn with the rose
You must take as it grows,
No thorn without roses brings joy to the nose,
And they only are wise who can cunningly join
Religion and beauty, wit, wisdom, and wine!

III.

'Twas yesterday only, myself and St. Paul,
When vespers were over, sat sipping our nectar,
There came up from earth to the heavenly hall
A lean-visaged fellow, as pale as a spectre;
A cross on his breast,
And a rope round his vest,
And a skull in his hand very plainly confessed

That he knew not in mystical wedlock to join
With piety pleasure, and wisdom with wine!

IV.

Such fellows I hate: so I said, in this place
All cherubs are rosy, no seraph is yellow;
We don't measure worth by the length of the face,
So sit down with Paul and with me, and be mellow!
With hollow surprise
He broadened his eyes,
And held up his hand for a sign to the skies,
Showing plainly he knew not the cunning to join
Religion with reason, and wisdom with wine.

V.

To this self-tormentor what after befell,
Who looked like a lemon, when nectar was flowing,
If he went back to earth, or was trapped into hell,

I really don't know, and 'tis not worth the knowing.
Myself and St. Paul,
When on earth's cloudy ball,
Were never found lagging when duty did call;
We stood for our faith, where our life was the fine,
But we never looked sour on a glass of good wine!

VI.

And now my discourse you have heard to the end,
My name you may use, and you know the condition,
If wisely you temper and skilfully blend
The hard-headed Scot with the quick-witted Grecian;
Myself and St. Paul,
From the bright azure hall,
Will bring your petitions and wait on your call,
And teach you to mingle in harmony fine
A song with a sermon, and wisdom with wine.

A Song of Summer.

'Always in your darkest hours strive to remember your brightest.'

J. P. RICHTER.

SING me a song of Summer,
For my heart is wintry sad,
That glorious bright new-comer,
Who makes all Nature glad!
Sing me a song of Summer,
That the dark from the bright may borrow,
And the part in the radiant whole of things
May drown its little sorrow!

Sing me a song of Summer,
When God walks forth in light,
And spreads his glowing mantle
O'er the blank and the grey of the night;

And where he comes, his quickening touch
  Revives the insensate dead,
And the numbed and frozen pulse of things
  Beats music to his tread.

Sing me a song of Summer,
  With his banners of golden bloom,
That glorious bright new-comer,
  Who bears bleak winter's doom,
With banners of gold and of silver,
  And wings of rosy display,
And verdurous power in his path,
  When he comes in the pride of the May;

When he comes with his genial sweep
  O'er the barren and bare of the scene,
And makes the stiff earth to wave
  With an ocean of undulant green;
With flourish of leafy expansion,
  And boast of luxuriant bloom,

And the revel of life as it triumphs
  O'er the dust and decay of the tomb.

Sing me a song of Summer;
  O God! what a glorious thing
Is the march of this mighty new-comer
  With splendour of life on his wing!
When he quickens the pulse of creation,
  And maketh all feebleness strong,
Till it spread into blossoms of beauty,
  And burst into pæans of song!

Sing me a song of Summer!
  Though my heart be wintry and sad,
The thought of this blessed new-comer
  Shall foster the germ of the glad.
'Neath the veil of my grief let me cherish
  The joy that shall rush into day,
When the bane of the winter shall perish
  In the pride and the power of the May.

Farewell to Summer.

I HEARD the whistling North wind say
When it came down with power,
Athwart the russet ferny brae,
And by the old grey tower:
I heard the whistling North wind say,
Bright Summer suns no more
Shall shine on Oban's dimpled bay,
And green Dunolly's shore.

I saw a fox-glove in the dell
Beneath the crag so grey,
One lonely, lean, belated bell,
And thus it seemed to say:

The glory of the June is past,
  My purple kin are gone,
And I am left a poor outcast
  To die in the cold alone !

I saw the long black ragged cloud
  O'ercap the frowning Bens,
And trails of thick blue mist enshroud
  The green far-gleaming glens ;
And thus the black cloud seemed to say,
  Now Summer suns are dim,
The stout old Winter holds his sway,
  And I will reign with him.

And is it so ?—brightest of things,
  God's beauty-vested Summer,
Shall it depart on hasty wings
  That was so late a comer
And I who lived with fragrant breeze,
  Blue skies, and purple braes,

On hueless flowers and leafless trees
  Must feed my widowed gaze?

It may not be : up ! let us go !
  I will not stay and look
Where gorgeous Nature's pictured show
  Is now a blotted book.
Let Nature die ! She'll live again
  When six dull months expire ;
Meanwhile against both wind and rain
  Heap we the blazing fire,

Snug in the chambered town ! and call
  My troop of friends together,
And for six months let no word fall
  Of Nature, wind, or weather;
And ply the work of thought or art
  That helps both self and neighbour,
And sing with glad and guileless heart
  The song that seasons labour.

And bring the grey tomes from the shelves
  And learn strong will from Cato,
And take high value of ourselves
  From lofty-thoughted Plato:
And, while with friendly cheer we pass
  The rare, rich-blooded bottle,
Give learnèd flavour to the glass
  By saws from Aristotle!

And then we 'll talk of Church and State,
  And wish the hangman's rope
To wed their necks to righteous Fate
  Who love the Roman Pope!
And blame the loons who gave the sway
  To the mere polled majority,
With clamorous yells to overbray
  The voice of grave authority.

And then,—why then, we 'll go to bed,
  And wake, above all sorrow

Of factious brawls to lift our head,
  By faithful work to-morrow,—
Work through long weeks of blustering storm,
  And Winter's gloomy reign,
Till the great pulse of things grow warm,
  And Nature lives again.

And suns shall shine, and birds shall sing,
  And odorous breezes blow,
And ferns uncurl their folded wing
  Where star-eyed flowerets grow;
And surly blasts shall cease to bray,
  And stormy seas to roar
On Oban's warm sun-fronting bay,
  And green Dunolly's shore.

A Song of the Country.

Written near Witley, in Surrey.

AWAY from the roar and the rattle,
  The dust and the din of the town,
Where to live is to brawl and to battle,
  Till the strong treads the weak man down!
Away to the bonnie green hills
  Where the sunshine sleeps on the brae,
And the heart of the greenwood thrills
  To the hymn of the bird on the spray.

Away from the smoke and the smother,
  The veil of the dun and the brown,
The push and the plash and the pother,
  The wear and the waste of the town!

Away where the sky shines clear,
  And the light breeze wanders at will,
And the dark pine-wood nods near
  To the light-plumed birch on the hill.

Away from the whirling and wheeling,
  And steaming above and below,
Where the heart has no leisure for feeling,
  And the thought has no quiet to grow.
Away where the clear brook purls,
  And the hyacinth droops in the shade,
And the wing of the fern uncoils
  Its grace in the depth of the glade.

Away to the cottage so sweetly
  Embowered 'neath the fringe of the wood,
Where the wife of my bosom shall meet me
  With thoughts ever kindly and good.
More dear than the wealth of the world,
  Fond mother with bairnies three,

And the plump-armed babe that has curled
  Its lips sweetly pouting for me.

Then away from the war and the rattle
  The dust and the din of the town,
Where to live is to brawl and to battle
  Till the strong treads the weak man down
Away where the green twigs nod
  In the fragrant breath of the May,
And the sweet growth spreads on the sod,
  And the blithe birds sing on the spray.

A Song of Fatherland by a Traveller.

AIR—*Ho! are ye sleeping, Maggie?*

I 'VE wandered east, I 've wandered west,
In gipsy-wise a random roamer;
Of men and minds I 've known the best,
Like that far-travelled king in Homer.
But O! for the land that bore me,
O! for the stout old land
Of breezy Ben and winding glen,
And roaring flood, and sounding strand!

I 've seen the domes of Moscow far,
In green and golden glory gleaming;
And stood where sleeps the mighty Czar,
By Neva's flood so grandly streaming.
But O! *etc.*

I 've stood on many a storied spot,
  Where blood of heroes flowed like rivers,
Where Deutschland rose at Gravelotte,
  And dashed the strength of Gaul to shivers.
    But O ! *etc.*

I 've stood where stands in pillared pride,
  The shrine of Jove's spear-shaking daughter,
And humbled Persia stained the tide
  Of free Greek seas with heaps of slaughter.
    But O ! *etc.*

I 've stood upon the rocky crest,
  Where Jove's proud eagle spreads his pinion,
Where looked the God far east, far west,
  And all he saw was Rome's dominion.
    But O ! *etc.*

I 've fed my eyes by land and sea,
  With sights of grandeur streaming o'er me,

But still my heart remains with thee,
  Dear Scottish land, that stoutly bore me.
    O! for the land that bore me,
    O! for the stout old land,
    With mighty Ben, and winding glen,
    Stout Scottish land, my own dear land!

A Song of Freemasonry.

I.

GOD save me! at last the grim waste I have passed
  Of a prickly scholastic theology,
And now in a region I float, where religion
  To common sense owes no apology.
But pray don't expect I shall found a new sect,
  No pulpit on earth I've an eye to!
My new patent plan's to be merely a man,
  And as I was born live and die too!
        Orthodox, heterodox,
        Luther, and Laud, and Knox,
      Squabbles of High Church and Low Church

'Tis my present plan
To be merely a MAN,
And laugh both at High Church and Low
Church!

II.

I looked and I wondered, I battled and blundered
With much metaphysical struggle,
With saintly desiring, and pious aspiring,
Till reason itself seemed a juggle.
And now the poor swimmer, with every vain glimmer
Of hope sank more deep than before, Sir!
Till I fell on this notion of healthy devotion,
That a man is a man, and no more, Sir!
Orthodox, heterodox,
Luther, and Laud, and Knox,
Squabbles of High Church and Low Church!
If no wisdom you see
In my masonry free,
Then go to the High or the Low Church!

III.

'Tis new, and 'tis old, to no Churchman 'tis sold,
This gospel all true hearts believe it,
And blessed are they, 'mid the sons of the clay,
Who with hearty good welcome receive it.
O ! seek not a spell from the dark depths of hell,
Nor let not the bright starry host win you !
The gospel of God is at no bishop's nod,
'THE KINGDOM OF HEAVEN IS WITHIN YOU'!
Orthodox, heterodox,
Luther, and Laud, and Knox,
Vain wisdom of High and of Low Church ;
Though the cock on the steeple
Is gilt for the people,
And bells ring for High and for Low Church!

IV.

A poor Arab maid may with faith undismayed,
Her heart in the desert sustain, Sir !

And a Christian may tread on a poor brother's head,
  And all for most heathenish gain, Sir!
In Christian and Turk the deep Devil may lurk,
  In Kaiser and Tartary Khan, Sir!
But I know a spell that will blast him to hell,
  'Tis to swear by the GOD that's in MAN, Sir!
        Orthodox, heterodox,
        Luther, and Laud, and Knox,
      Harsh dogmas of High Church and Low
          Church.
        For what's in a name?
        'Tis smoke round the flame
      To bemuddle both High Church and Low
          Church.

V.

      nal decrees and election I can
  Know as much and as little as you, Sir!
But that I'm a man who can purpose and plan,
  'Tis true, by the Powers, 'tis true, Sir!

And 'tis my intention, I modestly mention,
  To cleave to my kin and my clan, Sir!
And do some small good to the brave brotherhood
  That graces the title of man, Sir!
      Orthodox, heterodox,
    Luther, and Laud, and Knox,
    Mere quibbles of High Church and Low Church!
      Your wits run aground,
      Or in misty profound,
    You are swamped by the High and the Low Church!

VI.

My fancy bright weaves it, my firm faith believes it,
  The time is not far, but is near, now!
When strong hearts with glee shall shake their wings free
  From crotchets and whims that are dear now!

When every true man shall bless brother man
  By Bible-law and by Koran, Sir!
And each true heart brim with free worship to Him
  Whose image shines brightest in MAN, Sir!
      Orthodox, heterodox,
      Luther, and Laud, and Knox,
    Vain squabbles of High Church and Low
        Church!
      In God and in Man
      I believe; but I can
    Subscribe to sheer nonsense in no Church!

A Revolutionary Ode.

'*I will overturn, overturn, overturn it!*'—EZEKIEL.
'*Break up your fallow ground, and sow not among thorns.*'
JEREMIAH.

I DID dream a bodeful dreaming;
Thunders rolled, red fires were gleaming,
Earth did quake.
And I saw God's angel winging
Earthward, earnest message bringing;
Fearful in my ears 'tis ringing:
Thus he spake:

'Rouse thee, Wrath, and be a giant!
People's Will, that hath been pliant
Long, too long,

Up! and snap the rusty chaining,
Brittle bond for thy restraining;
Know the hour; the weak are reigning;
Thou art strong.

'Rise, and right the wrongs of ages,
Balance Time's unequal pages
With the sword!
Velvet-cushioned fools have slumbered,
Wanton weeds my garden cumbered;
Now their barren days are numbered,
Saith the Lord.

'Hear, ye loveless, narrow-hearted,
Few for whom the many smarted,
Hear my word!
I have heard the people's moaning,
I have known the poor man's groaning,
I have vowed a red atoning,
Saith the Lord!

'Who have lived in pillowed pleasure,
Ye shall now, in righteous measure,
Eat the dust;
Who beheld the bondman sallow
Pine, that ye in lust might wallow,
Ye shall fat young Freedom's fallow!
So 'tis just.

'People's heroes, mountain-breasted,
Looking lightnings, tempest-crested,
Seize the sword
Bellow with a vengeful thunder,
Turn each topmost over under,
Let Pride's purple minions wonder,
Saith the Lord!

'For their hopes a strong delusion,
For their plans a dark confusion,
I have stored;

Pride with folly shall be mated,
Wisdom still shall come belated,
Mercy shall not find the fated,
                                        Saith the Lord!

'Iron men and unrelenting,
Who shall do, without repenting,
                                        Deeds abhorred,
For my vengeance I have chosen;
Them no wheedling words shall cozen
They are hard, their tears are frozen,
                                        Saith the Lord!

'Sudden fear shall seize the palace;
Every wile of witless malice
                                        Shall be tried.
Things despised, the weak, the nameless,
I will fire with fury tameless;
They shall smite, themselves not blameless,
                                        Blameful pride.

'Kings shall meet and band together,
Despot spread for despot brother
Solemn board.
What they vow they shall pursue it,
I will spur and goad them to it;
They shall do; I will undo it,
Saith the Lord!

'March, mine elect iron warriors!
Strike! and old Pride's jealous barriers
Stand no more.
Ye shall judge the kings with rigour,
Ope the lists to strength and vigour;
Earth her increase to the digger
Shall restore.

'Tear the patch-work, rend the rotten
Let the useless be forgotten,
Earth the dead!

Time 'tis none for square and bevel,
Those I send shall raze and level;
Terror through the courtly revel
They shall spread!

'Wit I sent—the fools did scoff it;
Love they knew not; now my prophet
Is the SWORD.
With stern hate I have begun it;
When strong Love hath bravely won it,
They shall know that I have done it,
Saith the Lord!'

Spake the God-sent, thunder-knelling,
Feeble hearts of men compelling,
And upsoared.
I with salvèd sight awaking,
In swift ruin's overtaking,
In the firm Earth's fearful quaking,
Knew the Lord.

A Dirge.

AIR—*Vom hoh'n Olymp.*

I.

AND is she gone; lost, lost to us for ever,
Gone back to mystery and to God,
And shall we look upon her beauty never,
Laid 'neath the cold unfeeling sod?
Pour the sharp sorrow, 'tis human to mourn,
Never, O never, the Dead may return!

II.

O she was fair, to nice completeness rounded,
Soft as a flower, bright as a star,

Of every diverse human good compounded,
  To make choice music without jar!
    Pour, *etc.*

III.

Now she is gone; Earth quits her grace for ever,
  And native Heaven reclaims his child,
Bright mirror of the glory of the Giver,
  In stainless radiance undefiled.
    Pour, *etc.*

IV.

O my lean eyes! she 's hid, she 's hid for ever,
  Dark, dark with mystery and with God;
And all my weeping can recall her never,
  Back from the cold unfeeling sod!
    Pour the sharp sorrow, 'tis human to mourn,
    Never on Earth the lost Dead may return!

Advice to a favourite Student on leaving College.

DEAR youth, grey books no blossoms bear;
Thou hast enough of learning;
For life's green fields thy march prepare,
And take my friendly warning.
I would not have thee longer stay,
To read of others' striving;
Wield thine own arm!—the only way
To know life is by living.

The brain's a small part of a man;
Though thought has wide dominions,
Thou canst not lift the smallest stone
By Speculation's pinions.

Who learns an art by lifeless rule,
  Through mists will still be blinking;
The subtlest thinker is a fool,
  Who spins mere webs of thinking.

The times are feverish; mark me well!
  Have faith and patience by thee;
Unless thou curl into thy shell,
  Thou 'lt find enough to try thee.
But that 's a weak device. I know
  Thou 'lt face it free and fearless;
But O! beware the greater foe,
  A spirit proud and prayerless!

I love a bold and venturous boy,
  Who, full of fresh emotion,
Launches with large and liberal joy
  On life's wide-rolling ocean.

But there are rocks; and blind to steer
  Were thoughtless folly's merit:
Curb thou thy force with holy fear,
  And keep a watchful spirit.

Where eager crowds contend for pelf,
  The seller and the buyer,
Each one free range seeks for himself,
  And cares for nothing higher.
Make honey in an ordered hive,
  Nor join the lawless scramble
Of men, with whom in life to thrive
  Is with good luck to gamble.

We live in days when all would climb
  With hot, high-strung employment;
Some rage in prose, some writhe in rhyme,
  All hate a calm enjoyment.

Freedom 's the watchword of the hour;
  But O! 'tis melancholy
When every bubbling brain has power
  To drown calm thought with folly!

The age is full of talkers. Thou
  Be silent for a season,
Till slowly-ripening facts shall grow
  Into a stable reason.
Pert witlings fling crude fancies round,
  As wanton whim conceits them,
Pleased when from fools the echoed sound
  Of their own folly greets them.

Nurse thou, where eager babble spreads,
  A quiet brooding nature,
Nor strive, by lopping taller heads,
  To raise thy lesser stature.

Eschew the cavilling critic's art,
  The lust of loud reproving ;
The brain by knowledge grows, the heart
  Is larger made by loving.

All things we cannot know. At sea
  As when a good ship saileth,
Our steps within the planks are free,
  Beyond all cunning faileth.
So man as by a living bond
  Of circling powers is bounded ;
Within the line is ours, beyond
  The sharpest wit 's confounded.

What thing thou knowest, nicely know
  With curious fine dissection ;
The smallest mite can something show
  That chains thy rapt inspection.

Allwhere with holy caution move,
  In God thy life is moving;
All things with reverent patience prove,
  'Tis God's will thou art proving.

What thing thou doest, bravely do;
  When Heaven's clear call hath found thee,
Follow!—with fervid wheels pursue,
  Though thousands bray around thee!
Yet keep thy zeal in rein; despise
  No gentle preparation;
Flash not God's truth on blinking eyes,
  With reckless inspiration!

Farewell, my brave, my bright-eyed boy!
  And from the halls of learning,
Thy face, my long familiar joy,
  Take, with this friendly warning.

And when with weighty truth thou 'rt fraught
  From Life, the earnest preacher,
Think sometimes with a kindly thought
  On me, thy faithful teacher.

The Garden:

TO A YOUNG LADY ON HER BIRTHDAY.

MAIDEN, on thy father's garden
Thou dost look, and thou dost see
Growths of green and golden beauty
Many, but their types are three;
One the tree, the strong, tall-bodied,
Branching forth with arms of power,
One with foodful root or fruitage,
One with fragrant-blooming flower.

Maiden, all things are a symbol;
Tree, and flower, and foodful weed
Quaintly preach a pictured lesson,
If thine eyes are wise to read.

Lend thy hearing; sixty summers
Not in vain have wisdomed me;
I will show thee what the garden
Quaintly teaches me and thee.

In the tree behold thy father;
Strongly built is he to stand
In the brunt of life unshaken
With an eye of cool command.
In the tempest's face he tosses
Forth his arms; and gentle things
Gather round his bole, and glory
In the lordship of his wings.

In the foodful herb, thy mother
Finds meet symbol, by whose care
All the household fed and nourished
Stands so firm, and shows so fair.

She is toiling late and early,
Working where no eye can see,
Like the root, 'neath earthy covert
Growing healthful food for thee.

And thou, laughing Henrietta,
What remains for thee? the flower;
Growth the fairest and the sweetest
In the green redundant bower.
And the flower with fragrant blossom
That so aptly symbols thee,
What with pictured text it preaches
Hear, thou dainty maid, from me.

Youth is lovely; cherish beauty;
'Tis thy dower; not in vain
God with lavish blooms of beauty
Spanned the slope, and sowed the plain.

Goodness is the soul of beauty;
Cherish goodness; it will shine
Through the glooms of life the darkest,
Like bright rubies in a mine.

Loveliest flowers have sweetest fragrance;
Let sweet fragrance flow from thee,
Vivid breath of pure emotion,
Flame from smoky passion free.
Lowly reverence, gentle pity,
Every gracious thought benign
From the loving heart of woman
That makes human life divine.

Maiden, thou hast heard the lesson,
As my tongue had strength to tell,
Typed for thee, in flowery garden;
Take it now, and use it well.

Wingèd words are lightly spoken,
With the breath the sermon dies;
But the precept of the moment
Tasks a lifetime to the wise.

The Wisdom of Life.

WOULD you lead a happy life,
Free from melancholy,
Gnawing care and thorny strife,
And plunges of blind folly—
I will tell you how to live
Heartily and truly,
With sweet honey in your hive,
Like a bee in July.

Like the bee, be out and work
When the sun is shining,
Never in a corner lurk,
Whimpering and whining.

If you scour the fields, you 'll find
Thyme, or mint, or clover;
Something to a willing mind
God will still discover.

When the sky is grim and grey,
Though the clouds rain fountains,
March; and molehills on your way
Don't mistake for mountains.
If a ghost beside you stand,
Make no fearful comment;
But face the shadow boldly, and
'Tis vanished in a moment!

What the folks of you may say
Never mind a rattle,
Spin your quiet yarn, while they
Waste their wind in battle.

Lies that float on windy wings
  With windy haste will perish;
But the seed of truthful things
  Time's fruitful womb will cherish.

Hold your head erect, but not
  Haughtily, to all men;
When your fair fame they would blot,
  Never answer small men.
When they spring with hissing harm,
  Madder still and madder,
Shake them gently from your arm,
  As Paul let drop the adder.

Storms will have their gusty way,
  Fools will have their ranting;
But sense outrides the roughest day,
  And sees the end of canting.

Wrap your mantle round your breast,
  And when the storm is loudest,
Lightly fling your brightest jest
  And let your gait be proudest.

Wouldst thou Truth's fair semblance see,
  All viewless to the rabble,
Keep thy soul unbribed and free
  From Whig and Tory squabble ;
From fretful faction's hoarse debate,
  From foiled ambition's canker,
From seas of never-ending prate,
  And floods of sacred rancour.

Let your eye range freely round
  To spell the scroll of Nature ;
But ever with an awe profound
  Revere the great Creator.

Let no phrase thy wit delude,
Let no dogma fetter;
But though to know all things is good,
To love all things is better.

Wear your heart not on your sleeve;
But on just occasion
Let men know what you believe
With breezy ventilation;
Prove the good, and make them thine,
With warm embrace and ample;
But never cast your pearls to swine,
Who turn and rend and trample.

Make a penny when you can,
'Tis useful as a tool is,
But who says, *Money makes the man*,
A meagre-witted fool is.

Rich is he whose genial breast,
With liberal salutation,
Hath welcomed all that 's bright and best
Throughout the wide creation.

When you 've got a willing steed,
Use it meek and mildly :
Soon the best will slack his speed
If you spur him wildly.
Race not with a ramping might,
Like puffy Boreas blowing ;
But like the glorious lord of light,
Be gentle in thy going.

Now my Muse must clip her wing—
Rhyme 's a fluent preacher ;
But how to do the proper thing
Life 's the only teacher.

Only he may know who tries ;
  And if you now determine
So to do as I advise,
  You'll never rue the sermon.

www.ingramcontent.com/pod-product-compliance
Lightning Source LLC
LaVergne TN
LVHW010251110826
845151LV00004B/1444